PERMANENT
way to
Good Health

SWADESH KOHLI

Nita Mehta Publications

Corporate Office
3A/3, Asaf Ali Road, New Delhi 110 002
Phone: +91 11 2325 2948, 2325 0091
Telefax: +91 11 2325 0091
E-mail: nitamehta@nitamehta.com
Website: www.nitamehta.com

Editorial and Marketing office
E-159, Greater Kailash II, New Delhi 110 048

Food Styling and Photography by Snab
Typesetting by National Information Technology Academy
3A/3, Asaf Ali Road, New Delhi 110 002

Recipe Development & Testing:
Nita Mehta Foods - R & D Centre
3A/3, Asaf Ali Road, New Delhi - 110002
E-143, Amar Colony, Lajpat Nagar-IV, New Delhi - 110024

Distributed by :
NITA MEHTA BOOKS
3A/3, Asaf Ali Road, New Delhi - 02
Distribution Centre :
D16/1, Okhla Industrial Area, Phase-I,
New Delhi - 110020
Tel.: 26813199, 26813200
E-mail: nitamehta.mehta@gmail.com

Editors:

Nita Mehta
Anurag Mehta

Price: Rs. 250/-

Acknowledgements

I thank my husband, Pran Nath Kohli, my daughters Nita Uppal and Abha Narang, my son and my daughter-in-law Vinit and Sonia Kohli for giving me moral support and encouragement during the compiling of my experiences in my life.

I want to mention my special gratitude, to my niece and her husband, Payal and Arvind Arora for their help and guidance.

My foremost thanks and appreciation to my brother and sister-in-law, Subhash and Nita Mehta, for encouraging me to write and then, publishing my books. My nephew and his wife, Anurag and Tanya, in helping me format the book.

My special thanks to my son-in-law, Manoj Uppal and my grand-daughters, Megha and Nikita Uppal for helping me to format this book and to get and assemble the pictures of the exercises.

Last but not the least, I am very much indebted to my late mother who brought me up with the knowledge of natural cure and my late mother-in-law who opened my mind towards the spiritual part.

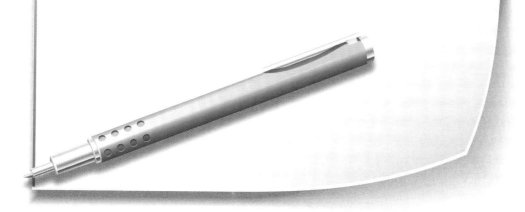

CONTENTS

LIFESTYLE
FOR
OPTIMUM HEALTH

FOOD POWER

There's no denying the fact that if you want to feel well and look well, you have to eat well. Food provides essential nutrients to repair, maintain and constantly renew the body. Diet should be simple, nutritious and balanced. **There is no single food that is a magic bullet against disease.** Eating a wide variety of foods like dark green, or bright colored fruits and vegetables, nuts, beans and high fiber whole grain breads and cereals, keeps you healthy. It creates a smooth flow of energy which circulates in the whole body and keeps it healthy. The body needs energy and energy is supplied by the food you eat.

The older we get, the more free radicals we produce, which play a central role in virtually every disease — cardiovascular disease like stroke and arteriosclerosis, Parkinson's disease, Alzheimer's, and type II diabetes. Research has proved that the various foods work at the cellular level, especially antioxidant rich fruits and vegetables, which are powerful medicine in the fight against cellular ageing.

Antioxidants are substances that bind with free radicals and prevent them from damaging cells. These antioxidants are abundant in colourful fruits and vegetables — spinach, broccoli, red apples, cranberries, blueberries, cherries and grapes. Servings recommended are 5 helpings of fruits and vegetables a day. This will protect your body and brain from the ill effects of ageing.

The fruits, juices and herbs are supercharged with natural burning fuel for good health. Fresh coriander chutney, mint chutney, basil pesto are all delicious ways to consume herbs. Mix half cucumber and half carrot when juicing sweet lime (mausami) or oranges to get benefits of both vegetable and fruit.

HEALING COLOURS
OF
VEGETABLES & FRUITS

Veggies are not only greens. Mix them with a variety of shades such as red, yellow, orange and purple and each color brings a new set of vitamins and minerals to the dish. Vitamin supplements cannot be compared to real food. The supplements are not well absorbed by the body, nor do they take the place of real food. It has been proved that taking separate nutrients in pill form can never compare to eating real whole foods.

The color of raw food benefits your body and psyche. But the color of food can benefit you only when taken raw or steamed, never over cooked. Different colors have different significances and are associated with certain organs...

RED

Red color in fruits and vegetables is for energizing the body. An emotionally intense color, it uplifts your spirits and pulls you out of depression. It reduces the risk of heart disease and blood disorders. Carrots, beets, watermelon, red pepper, cherry are in the red color category.

GREEN

Calming green color compliments red, it is found in cabbage, spinach, guava, and grape. This color prevents cancer and cardio-vascular diseases, also soothes the nerves.

WHITE

Neutralizing White is neutral color. Is used to make a new beginning, evokes purity and cleanliness and brings about mental clarity. Cauliflower, potato, onion come under this color.

BLUE and PURPLE

Peaceful blue and purple are serene colours. Examples are found in blueberry, blue plum, purple cabbage, black-currant. This color is for curing throat problems and evoking a sense of tranquility. It is good for sleeping disorders and for heart, blood pressure and eye problems. Also, it helps in healthy ageing.

YELLOW

Merry yellow increases your metabolism, enhances concentration. This color is beneficial for all the endocrine system and for intestines. Examples are sweet lime, yellow pepper and mango.

ORANGE

Cheerful orange compliments blue, and is good for digestive system as well as the sexual organs. These foods are great anti-oxidants and toxin eliminators. They make you feel sociable and willing to try new things. Examples are pumpkin, and all citrus fruits like oranges, grapefruit, tangerines etc.

VIOLET

Violet and indigo are sobering colors which complement yellow. Soothing colors make one feel sober and sedate, also associated with spirituality. They help in mental disorders and prevent head/scalp diseases. Also are excellent memory booster. Examples are found in blackberry, eggplant, black grapes.

Wheat and rice are staples in most diets but there are many more varieties of grain waiting to get their due...

Pearl Millet

Also known as: *bajra*

This is the fourth most important grain in India grown mostly in Rajasthan, Gujarat, Maharashtra and Uttar Pradesh. It is consumed in the same way as rice after de-husking. It is being touted as the most healthy alternative to wheat.

Health Quotient: *Bajra* is highly nutritious, non-glutinous and easy to digest. It is a warming grain so helps heat the body in cold or rainy seasons and cold climates.

Used to Make: rotis, namkeens, diet food, porridge.

Finger Millet

Also known as: *ragi, nachani*

Like bajra, ragi is the next big thing in health food with ragi breakfast cereals, khakhras, rotis and namkeens hitting the market. This red-coloured grain has a hard seed coat and is used in whole-meal form. This grain must be hulled before it can be used for human consumption.

Health Quotient: It's high in protein and calcium and low in carbohydrates. It is a good flour substitute for diabetics.

Used to Make: bhakris, rotis, khakhras, bread, chaklis, baby food.

Maize

Also known as: makka/makkai

Popularly known as corn, maize was introduced to the world by sailors from Spain and Portugal, a produce of South and Central America. The small golden coloured kernels produce cornflour, cornmeal and are also consumed whole.

Health Quotient: It's the only grain that contains vitamin B & is also a source of vitamin C and iron. It is also gluten-free.

Used to Make: Popcorn, tortilla chips, polenta, make ki roti

Oats

Also known as: jai

Whole oats when unprocessed are coated with nutritious bran but have to be rolled or ground as oatmeal or flaked before consumption. They top the charts as a healthy breakfast cereal. Available rolled, flaked, steel-cut, oatmeal and oat bran.

Health Quotient: high in soluble fibers, it contains vitamins E and B, iron and calcium.

Barley

Also known as: jau

It is believed to be the oldest cultivated grain with a mild, sweet flavour and chewy texture. It is a popular health food but is also used for malting and is a key ingredient in beer and whisky production.

Health Quotient: The cereal is high on fiber making it good for digestion. It is a rich source of calcium, phosphorus, iron, magnesium and vitamin B.

Used to Make: barley water, soups, stews, flour, porridge. Mix some barley flour with whole wheat flour to enhance the fibre of the chappatis.

Sorghum

Also known as: jowar

A king of millet, this is a staple in India, China and Africa. It is used much like rice or in ground form as flour. The flour may also be made into a thin porridge, a thick paste of dough by boiling in water. Some varieties can also be popped.

Health Quotient: it contains iron, calcium and potassium and is gluten-free.

Used to Make: jowari rotis, bhakris, biscuits, porridge, bread.

Rye

A popular grain closely related to barley and wheat. It can be eaten whole, either as boiled berries, or rolled, like oats.

Health Quotient: It is a good source of vitamins B and E, protein, calcium, iron and potassium

Used to Make: bread, muffins, flour, rye beer, whiskey, vodka.

IMMUNITY BOOSTERS

It is advisable to boost your Immune System to prevent any sort of ill health. The best way to do this is the natural way.

Immune system is the body's disease fighting net-work of cells. These cells travel the entire body, contacting virtually every other cell. They recognize, they attack - defending the body against micro-infected cells. To boost the immune system...

- ✓ Add plenty of ginger and garlic in your cooked food. Ginger root has pain relieving properties.

- ✓ Drink 2-4 glasses of hot water every hour. Take thyme herbal tea thrice a day for cold and during flu.

- ✓ ½ tsp of turmeric in a glass of milk taken before going to bed can boost immunity and increase stamina. (see page 28)

- ✓ Eat light meals, especially dinner.

- ✓ Drink warm concoction of cardamom, fennel, cumin, ginger in the form of tea.

- ✓ Rest enough so that body can fight the infection.

- ✓ Drink juice of amla, carrots and tomatoes, which is rich in vitamin C.

- ✓ Once a week do full body massage. This will boost blood circulation and immunity. Massage really helps to remove pain in the tired legs and hips.

- ✓ Eat nuts especially walnuts, pistachios & almonds.

- ✓ Tulsi tea is good for viral and respiratory infections. It energizes body cells and helps increase stamina. Tulsi can be taken with honey for cough.

ABOUT FATS

Fat is Essential – like Carbohydrates

Don't think of fat as harmful unless you are referring to processed fats as margarine, fried foods and commercially produced vegetable oils from which vitamin E has been removed. Fat in it's natural form and consumed in moderate amounts as a part of a balance diet is yet to be proven bad. Fat has valuable roles... Essential fatty acids boost the immune system and ward off diseases. Fat is needed to form cell membranes. It is also required for the absorption of fat soluble vitamins like A, D, E, K.

What kind of Fat?

(a) Saturated fats are those that are solid at room temperature, i.e. the fat in most meats and eggs, dairy products like butter, ghee and coconut oil. Saturated fats above recommended levels lead to fatty deposit in arteries, obesity, increase in cholesterol and triglycerides.

(b) Unsaturated fats are those that are liquid at room temperature i.e. olive, canola, sunflower, corn, fish oils and other vegetable oils.

The kind and quality of fat you eat is more important than the amount of fat you eat. Unsaturated ones are the best. The unsaturated ones can be further categorised as polyunsaturated fats (PUFA) and monounsaturated fats (MUFA). Olive oil is considered the healthiest oil as it has the right balance of PUFA and MUFA which are heart friendly and reduce the bad cholesterol and triglycerides in the body. Canola oil is another very healthy oil like olive oil. Both these oils prevent heart diseases, high B.P., diabetes and brain haemorrhage.

Cooking with Oil

Frying oil should not be reused because constant reheating sets off a chemical reaction that can create FREE RADICALS. It is thus healthier to fry foods in small amounts of oil. Do not use the same oil for frying again and again. Add some fresh oil to the oil that has been used for frying and use it up in the general cooking. When fats are overly heated again and again, they turn toxic - become rancid and deteriorate our health.

Benefits of Omega 3 and 6 fatty acids

Of all the fats we consume, two fatty acids are essential i.e. linoleic acid (an omega - 6 fatty acid) and alpha-linoleic (an omega - 3 fatty acid). Omega -6 is found in all vegetable oils and most grains and beans and Omega - 3 is found in walnuts and salmon, tuna and other fatty fish. Our health will start deteriorating if we do not receive both of these fatty acids on a regular basis.

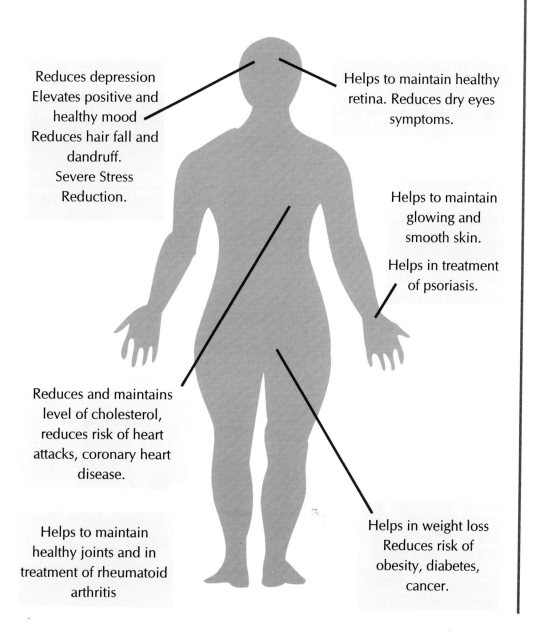

Reduces depression
Elevates positive and
healthy mood
Reduces hair fall and
dandruff.
Severe Stress
Reduction.

Helps to maintain healthy
retina. Reduces dry eyes
symptoms.

Helps to maintain
glowing and
smooth skin.

Helps in treatment
of psoriasis.

Reduces and maintains
level of cholesterol,
reduces risk of heart
attacks, coronary heart
disease.

Helps to maintain
healthy joints and in
treatment of rheumatoid
arthritis

Helps in weight loss
Reduces risk of
obesity, diabetes,
cancer.

BAD HEALTH HABITS

1. To eat on full stomach or eat quickly without chewing.

2. To eat more than your appetite.

3. Unbalanced diet, unhealthy diet.

4. To eat spiced food, lots of tea, coffee, sugar, white bread etc.

5. To eat under any type of tension like excitement, sorrow, anger, anxiety or hatred.

6. To sleep late and wake up late.

7. Fast irregular life.

8. To eat too much meat, drinking and smoking.

Foods contain thousands of micronutrients, many of which have not yet been identified by the nutritionists. So pills will not give what a bowl of cherries or a glass of carrot juice will. It has been found that individual foods contain different protective agents that help the body defend itself against illness. Some foods play a stronger role in preventing particular ailments than others.

A multivitamin does not fully make up for the missing nutrients in your diet. So, besides the multivitamin we should have nutritious well balanced food, specially the seniors above 50 years. One-a-day multiple vitamin formula supply some of the many nutrients. For health benefits vitamins and minerals need to work together. Nature combines them just in the right proportions. These foods cleanse the blood, which is the life of all flesh.

Unbalanced diet, unhealthy diet.

16

OPTIMUM HEALTH GUIDELINES

1. Eat servings of whole grain like whole wheat, brown rice, corn, oats, barley etc. every day. Mix wheat bran or oat bran with wheat flour for making chapatis.

2. Five servings of a variety of fresh fruits and vegetables, which make your diet rich in the anti-oxidants, will help prevent diseases.

3. Instead of butter/clarified butter like ghee/hydrogenated oils, it is safe to use canola oil or olive oil for cooking.

4. Proteins work best when taken from different sources, so the combination of grains, nuts, seeds and beans gives you all amino acids, which your body needs to rebuild itself.

5. Stick to regular pattern of eating and don't skip meals. Restrict your food choices when dinning out.

6. Avoid stimulants like tea, coffee, cokes and alcohol that put strain on the liver and affect its ability to flush out toxins. Opt for drinks like butter milk (lassi), vegetable and fruit juice instead. Fresh lemon mixed with water and honey is a good option too. Try adding fresh herbs like mint, coriander or basil to these drinks. They taste delicious! Reach out for a glass of water as frequently as you can.

7. Eat fresh food as much as possible, specially those which are in season. In winter for example, use cruciferous vegetables, green leafy vegetables and roots. In summer eat a variety of vitamin rich gourds (*tinda, tori, karela*).

8. Keep a positive attitude towards life. Do things that make you happy. Stay with family and friends. Stay active through work, play and community.

9. Do regular physical activity. Take time to walk 10 minutes every day, from your hectic schedule. Give importance to exercise as you would to an important meeting or appointment.

GOOD HEALTH FROM
Foods and Juices

Anise

Anise, this herb cures coughs, bronchial congestion and digestive problems, including heartburn and flatulence. Chew it as breath freshener. It contains chemicals that are similar to the female hormone estrogen. Anise is an excellent supplement for nursing mothers, because it will enrich their breast milk, and for women going through menopause, because it helps with the symptoms such as flashes.

Caraway

Caraway contains chemicals that have beneficial effect on muscles in the stomach, calming them and aiding in digestion. Its antispasmodic activity is effective in the relief of menstrual cramps.

Coriander

Coriander promotes gentle and effective digestion.

Garlic (lahsun)

(i)   Garlic is good for those who suffer from hypertension as it break the cholesterol in the blood, thus preventing the hardening of arteries.

(ii)   Garlic reduces body fat.

(iii)   A couple of cloves help ward off cancer.

(iv)   Fresh garlic when rubbed on pimples or ulcers, will make them disappear.

(v)   Boil 4 cloves of garlic in ½ cup milk, drink every night before going to bed. This will help asthma patients.

Ginger

(i)   Ginger quells nausea.

(ii)   It is used to fight cancer. Researchers, at the University of Michigan in Ann - Arbor, discovered that ginger has the ability to kill cancer cells in two ways: a. Apoptosis, in which the cancer cells, essentially commit suicide without harming surrounding cell. b. Auto-phagy, here the cells are trickled into digesting themselves (digestion of cellular constituents by enzymes of the same cell).

Turmeric

Turmeric has a number of beneficial healing properties. It has been long used in Ayurvedic medicine and in home remedies. It has been used as a stomach and skin tonic and blood purifier and for the treatment of skin diseases and wound healing.

(i) Suppressing the transformation and invasion of cancerous cells.

(ii) The rhizome of turmeric is highly aromatic and antiseptic. It also help in lowering blood cholesterol, internal blood clots and is beneficial in treating or reducing symptoms due to anti-tumor, anti-inflammatory, anti- bacterial effects.

(iii) Fresh turmeric rhizome juice when taken acts as an anthelmintic, a destroyer of parasites or worms especially of the stomach.

(iv) This herb protects bladder and gastro-intestinal cancers.

(v) When turmeric powder is put on an open bleeding wound, the blood stops immediately, and healing starts quickly without infection.

(vi) A paste of turmeric powder, raw onion slice and mustard oil, when this poultice is in place on a sprain it will reduce the swelling and the inflammation of the hurt, quicker than any other treatment.

(vii) ¼ tsp of roasted turmeric power taken orally can heal the internal wound, especially after the surgery.

(viii) Turmeric is very effective for internal wounds, especially in speeding post-operative healing.

Turmeric Recipe for Internal Wound Healing

Take, one teaspoon of clarified- butter (ghee) warm it up in a saucepan, add ½ teaspoon turmeric powder. Stir for a second then add one cup of milk. Bring it to a boil. Add sugar according to your taste. Let it cool a little then sip this hot drink slowly.

Turmeric Recipe for Rashes

(i) Take 2 teaspoonful turmeric powder, 2 teaspoonful ground carom seeds, and 2 teaspoons sugar in 4 glasses of water. Method: Boil it and reduce to 2 glasses. Drink one glass in the morning on empty stomach and one in the evening before sunset. Within 2-3 days the rashes will clear.

(ii) A paste of turmeric alone or combined with the pulp of neem leaves is used in ringworm, itching, eczema and other parasitic skin diseases.

Cold, cough, sore throat and congestion *can be cured by:*

(i) Taking turmeric in sweetened boiled milk.

(ii) Mix clarified butter with turmeric powder to relieve cough.

(iii) To sooth sore throat, suck a piece of turmeric rhizome and a little piece of jaggery.

(iv) Take 2 gm turmeric powder mix with 2 tsp of honey, twice a day to relieve congestion.

Fenugreek Seeds

Fenugreek Seeds Brew for Pain

Make a brew in 1 litre of boiling water putting 2 tablespoons of fenugreek seeds. Stir everything thoroughly. Cover the pot and reduce the heat let simmer the concoction for about 4 minutes. Let steep until the tea become lukewarm.

Honey

Heals wounds. Besides turmeric, honey is also found to have beneficial effects on wounds. The study in Britain, on 12 surgical patients, poured honey on the wounds of those patients, twice a day and covered with a light bandage. It was found that bacteria in the wounds disappeared completely within 3-6 days and complete healing occurred in all 12 patients within 8 weeks. One case took only three weeks to heal.

Cruciferous Vegetables

For getting the benefits of green vegetables without the infections, make soup of them or eat steamed vegetables. Cruciferous vegetables are used for cancer prevention and cure. Cruciferous vegetables like cabbage, cauliflower, brussels sprouts etc., release during cutting or chewing them will produce an antioxidant, Sulforaphane, which has cancer fighting killing effect.

Cranberry

Soak the painful blisters in pure cranberry juice. Much of your pain will go away immediately. The old blisters will go and the new ones will not hurt as much so long as you continue with cranberry soak. This treatment is very common among farmers, carpenters, loggers and weight lifters who tried the cranberry soak reported how quickly their blisters healed.

Chicory

Chicory is beneficial in skin care, liver ailment - sluggish liver, bile malfunction, even jaundice.

(i)   Chicory helps detoxify the body. Its high fiber content acts as a mild laxative. Chronic constipation can be effectively relieved just eating its leaves.

(ii) Chicory juice, when added to carrot and celery juice, has been seen to be beneficial for the bronchial passage and soothes Asthma.

(iii) Chicory when eaten along with celery and parsley, acts as a source of iron supplement.

(iv) Chicory is also a rich source of vitamin A and keeps eyes healthy.

Black Cumin Seeds

Black Cumin Seeds for Grey Hair

Factors for hair greying:

(i)   Faulty diet.

(ii) Lack of B vitamins, iron, copper and iodine in the daily diet.

(iii) Hereditary conditions.

(iv) Life style we lead; mental worries produce tension. Scalp cannot be nourished externally it can get the nutrients via blood stream. Both graying and thinning of hair may occur simultaneously since both are generally a result of ageing.

Other reasons for greying hair can be due to:

(i) Unclean condition of the scalp.

(ii) Washing -hair with hot water.

(iii) Drying hair with an electric dryer.

(iv) Use of hair dyes. Treatment for pre-maturing graying is more preventing than curative. Try to de-stress, and ensure that our lives are not too fast. Grey hair strands might just be an early warming of an internal imbalance.

Grey Hair Remedy: Take ½ cup black cumin seeds and ¼ cup sesame seeds grind them in a stone grinder or in a rolling mill. Boil in 2 cups of water on medium heat until only 1 cup remains. Rinse the hair with that every day after showering and leave the mixture in a bottle until the next time you bathe.

Do this **Massage for Hair Loss:** Bend your head down towards your knees and vigorously massage your scalp for 5 minutes. Brush on your head using a natural brush. Both these will stimulate circulation to bring more blood to the scalp to help nourish hair follicles.

Salt Water

Salt Water For Cysts

Acute cysts can be treated by home remedy: Mix 1 cup hot water with ¼ teaspoon salt, then dip a cotton ball in the solution and dab on the affected area. Let dry and repeat once daily. The heat from the water opens the infected pores, while the salt drains out the infection.

Benefits of Juices

Natural fruit sugars turn off your appetite and stop cravings. Healing vegetable and fruit juices make a perfect substitute for sweets and fatty foods. Experts say a glass of fresh fruit and vegetable juice daily give you all the nutrients you need to achieve the peak health, slow down the ageing process, eliminate arthritis pain, reduce the risk of heart attacks and stroke, boost your memory and pep up your sex life.

1. Cherry juice is acidic, it works well with arthritis and gout. Berries are also good for arthritis.

2. Pomegranate Juice: This juice, like carrot juice, is good for eyes.

3. Grape Juice: can tackle cholesterol, prevent heart attacks and strokes, and fight cancer.

4. Juice cucumber, bottle gourd, tomato and a carrot together to get a delicious juice for over all health.

5. 1 tbsp of gooseberry (*ambla*) juice mixed with 1 cup orange juice with ½ tsp rock salt and honey forms a natural expectorant. The salty action of this mixture on the lungs protects them from secondary infection during Cold and Flu.

6. A combination of equal parts of dark grape juice and apricot puree, when taken shows a noticeable reduction in the inflammation of the colon lining;

1 cup of Apple juice contains 115 calories

1 cup of orange juice contain 115 calories

1 cup of carrot juice contain 45 calories

HOME REMEDIES

MY AMAZING CAR ACCIDENT

and how well I recovered from it by natural therapies

The accident that took place was amazing. We were six passengers in the car at the time of accident. The car's speed was only 20 miles/hour when it banged in the standing car in front. All the passengers in the car escaped unharmed, including the driver. This could have happened to anybody without any serious consequences. But all of a sudden drops of blood started coming out from my forehead without any pain. This ended up with non- stop flow of blood. I tried to stop the blood by a clean hand towel, but it was all soaked till the ambulance arrived, which took only 15 minutes. A clean, thick surgical pad was put on the wound, but it had the same fate as the towel. In the emergency ward I was told that I had 3″ long cut which was quite deep. Luckily my skull was intact with no bone cracks.

The astonishing part of the accident was that there was no sharp article in the car, which could make such a deep and sharp wound. Amazingly, my glasses that I was wearing were thrown on the car floor without even a scratch on them.

It all seemed as if God ordain this on me so that I could experience the sufferings which one undergoes in such situations. Also, He gave me courage, patience, will-power and right instinct to take it in my hand **to treat myself by natural therapies like Yoga and other Natural Therapies and changed life style which included exercise, diet and weight control.** The aquatic exercise in the shower and in the bath-tub helped me in painless speedy recovery.

In the emergency ward, the surgeon, who stitched me up, did a marvelous job with the three layers of stitches he put in my head.

NATURAL PAIN RELIEF

After being discharged from the hospital I came home. Doctor prescribed pain- killers regularly for the pain and instructed my children to ensure that I was not avoiding the medicine and bearing the pain. But I did not feel unbearable pain, may be due to **Turmeric-milk home concoction (*haldi waala doodh*) and the fenugreek seeds brew.** I always avoided medicines as they often have side effects later. I want to share the recipes of these natural pain killers with my readers...

Turmeric Recipe for Internal Wound Healing

Take one teaspoon of clarified- butter (ghee) in a saucepan, warm it slightly and add ½ teaspoon turmeric powder. Stir for a second then add one cup of milk. Bring it to a boil. Add sugar according to your taste. Let it cool a little, then sip this hot drink slowly.

I started to take turmeric milk from the very first day of the accident. For the first two days I took twice and then once daily for six months, till I felt that my internal wounds were no longer there.

Fenugreek Seeds Brew for Pain

Make a brew in 1 ½ litres (7-8 cups) of boiling water and 2 tablespoons of fenugreek seeds (*methi daana*). Stir everything thoroughly. Bring to a boil. Cover the pot and reduce the heat. Let it simmer for about 4 minutes. Let steep until the tea becomes lukewarm. I took this fenugreek brew only for a week after my accident.

Effects of Accident & Natural Treatment

The first few days were a nightmare. In the first couple of days I had to change my bandage twice daily, applying Zinc antiseptic ointment on the wound, to prevent the stitches getting infected. The wound and stitches on the head took about 10 days to heal and I could dispense with the bandage then. I only applied the ointment for a few more days.

My head was swollen all over, and it was woolly and soft to the touch as if there were no bones or muscles in the swollen area. My face and neck were all covered with bruises. The medical reason given by the doctor was that whenever there is an injury in any part of the body, the body fluids rush to that injured area to protect against infection. As a result, **there is swelling and redness surrounding the injury. The bruise marks come afterwards because as the injury starts healing, the fluid start receding. The path on which this fluid tries to recede becomes a little swollen and blue and that is why black bruises appear.**

In my case the bruises came up to my forehead, face, neck down to the shoulder bone. The swelling took almost eight to nine months to heal. During the healing time the skin on my forehead, face and entire head was very dry.

I had to put **Gooseberry (Amla) hair oil** on my head daily to massage the hair and head, while **Vitamin E oil** took care of the wounded area on my forehead.

Vitamin E Oil to Remove Scars

For my scars the doctor advised me to put pure vitamin E oil on them, twice daily for a month and then once till the scars got dissolved. Doctor told me that her sister applied vitamin E on her wound and the scar was cleared, though it took time. It also proved effective in my case, after 7-8 months you could hardly make out where the wound was. I regularly massaged my wound with 2-3 drops of vitamin E oil, gently rubbing it into the scar, till it was absorbed. For my face doctor prescribed vitamin E moisturizing cream to be applied daily after bath. **Vitamin E has done wonders on me,** I have acquired my normal soft skin and only a faint mark of the scar is left, that can only be recognized if looked at attentively.

Ice Pack Treatment

For the dull area around the wound and a sharp pain starting from the wound to the back of the head intermittently, the doctor prescribed holding **an ice pack to it for**

twenty minutes, then give a break for two hours, then repeat after every two hours throughout the day for the first week.

After that I put ice pack once a day for 10 minutes in the following two weeks. This reduced my irritation and gave quite a relief to the swelling and pain in two months, but the area around the wound remained heavy and hard to the touch for a long time. At last now after almost a year the dullness has reduced much and the stretching of the nerve is just bare minimum.

Rest

Rest was also one of the major factors that helped me to recover in normal course of time without any complications, and regained my strength in minimum of time.

Some claim that dreams can heal.

Ancient scriptures worldwide describe dreams that brought insight and access to another reality.

At least 8 hours sleep is an essential factor to revitalize your body.

> **Physical trainers state that the human body operates on 12 hour cycles.** In many countries, including India, afternoon resting is a 'power nap' time. These kinds of siestas are said to regenerate cells, revive mental agility, and increase physical strength.

Food

> **Plants that strengthen bone rebuilding** are romaine lettuce, parsley, kale, watercress, endive, These dark leafy green vegetables are high in calcium, magnesium, potassium and boron. All of these minerals are necessary for healing injuries and bone building.

"What to eat, how to eat and what not to eat is a very important question today." I was always a staunch believer in the medicinal properties of food, so I was very careful about my diet.

Besides multivitamins, which can't fully compensate for all the plant nutrients, **I follow a healthy eating plan, based on balanced diet and moderate eating, drinking plenty of water.**

My diet was based on those vegetables which have healing properties and I took more quantity of liquid in the meal.

HERB POWER

Heal yourself with herbs! There's a healthy herb for every season and every reason.

Herbs are leaves of aromatic plants, rich in nutrients and minerals. They are also used for medicinal purposes as remedies for colds, flu, coughs, throat infections and pain.

Herbal Flavour to Your Food

Herbs are used as seasonings; they can reduce reliance on salt. Use them to give subtle or strong accents to soups, sauces, raitas, stews, casseroles, vegetables & cereals. Aroma is a good indicator of quality in both fresh and dried herbs. Crumbling a few leaves can test the scent of herbs. A weak or stale aroma indicates old, less potent herbs.

Though fresh is always best, herbs are often dried and powdered so that they can be consumed all year round. Don't overcook fresh herbs. When leafy greens are overcooked, they lose their chlorophyll as well as other nutrients. Cook on low flame for a happy green colour. For maximum iron, add a twist of lemon. Vitamin C helps absorption of iron!

Basil (Tulsi)

Key Nutrients: vitamin A and C, calcium, iron, magnesium, phosphorus, potassium.

Benefits: Basil helps treat headaches, dizziness, vertigo, stomach cramps, nausea and constipation. Basil oil is used to treat insect bites and minor cuts.

Did you know? Basil is a remedy for bronchitis and colds.

Bay Leaf (Tez Patta)

Key Nutrients: calcium, iron, magnesium, vitamin A, B, C and E.

Benefits: Bay leaves are used to treat stress and anxiety. They also improve digestion and help detoxify the system.

Did you know? Bay leaf oil is antibacterial. To repel household pests naturally, spread some crushed leaves in the kitchen.

Coriander Leaves (Hara Dhania)

Key Nutrients: vitamin A, B and C, iron, calcium, zinc.

Benefits: Coriander leaves are diuretic and help detoxify the system. They also help improve quality of blood, lower cholesterol levels and improve eyesight.

Mint (Pudina)

Key Nutrients: calcium, phosphorus, iron, vitamin A, C, and E.

Benefits: Mint is used as a treatment for indigestion, colic, heartburn and flatulence. It can also stimulate the appetite and cure nausea and headaches. Peppermint tea can help soothe a dry throat.

Did you know? Mint ointment is good for headaches. Mint is also used as flavour for mouthwash and toothpaste.

Dill (Soya ka Saag)

Key Nutrients: calcium, iron, magnesium, phosphorus, potassium vitamin A, C and E.

Benefits: Dill is used to treat colic, flatulence and indigestion. It is an effective appetite stimulant and helps stimulate milk in nursing mothers.

Oregano (Ajwain family)

Key Nutrients: calcium, iron, phosphorus, potassium, magnesium, vitamin A and C.

Benefits: Oregano has powerful antioxidant and anticancer properties. It aids digestion, helps to get rid of intestinal parasites, treats nausea and diaorrhea.

FOOD AS MEDICINE

Food for Maintaining Bones and Muscles

Diet plays an integral role in developing and maintaining bones and muscles. The extra calcium, which is not consumed, gets deposited on the joints, resulting in rheumatoid arthritis. Bones can pick up health and disturbed life functions may resume smoothly again, by planning calcium intake in your diet carefully.

Low calcium levels in the body can lead to abnormalities like joint pains, numbness in the arms and legs, besides other ailments. Adequate amount of calcium is very important.

Milk is a rich source of Calcium, but some people are lactose intolerant and do not have the enzymes that digest milk sugar lactose, leading to gastro-intestinal distress diarrhea and flatulence.

Alternate food sources of calcium and other nutrients:

1. **Sesame seeds** are one of the richest sources of Calcium. Sesame seeds oil is sometimes recommended to heart patients.

2. **Peanuts** are good source of calcium and protein.

3. **Raw tofu** is very good in correcting hormonal imbalance. Tofu can be stir fried with vegetables in soy sauce and ginger. It can be taken in salads.

4. **Dried figs** (2 figs) daily can boost body's immunity to infection. Good for constipation.

5. **Almonds** are good source of vitamin E.

6. **Chickpeas** soaked overnight, take it raw in salad. After cooking the calcium concentration is reduced significantly. It can produce gas.

Fragile Bones

If you've broken more than a couple of bones during your adult life, it could be possible your bones are weak due to lack of body's chief bone builder that is **vitamin D and calcium.**

You are not alone if you go by the myth that only women need calcium as they age. In fact men also need it especially if they eat larger amounts of meat, which is high in phosphorus and increases the body's need for calcium.

Solution

At breakfast drink a tall glass of milk (skim or light milk can be a better choice), have a cup of low fat yogurt with lunch or dinner and sneak in green leafy veggies, beans and whole channa into your diet whenever possible.

Dry Skin

If you have an itchy, dry scaly skin not just in winters but also through out the year, it may signal a lack of significant amount of **vitamin A**.

Dietary Solution

Every time you go to the market, make sure your basket contains at least two **orange** or **yellow** and two **dark green** vegetables or fruits. Spinach, mustard greens, tomatoes, melons, mangoes, apricots, carrots and sweet potatoes all have plenty of beta carotene, which is converted to vitamin A in the body. You can also get this vitamin directly from whole milk, egg yolk, cheese, fish oils but these sources have more fat and higher calories, so have less of these.

Vitamin A will not only give you a glowing and sparkling clear skin but also, as a bonus, promote good vision. It may also inhibit the development of certain tumors and increase the resistance to infection in children.

Lifeless Hair

In extreme cases your hair can lose its luster due to lack of sufficient intake of **proteins and iron** in your diet especially if you are dieting.

Solution

First of all do not just blindly go on a diet. Eat a good mix of foods. Concentrate on eating more fiber and incorporate some exercise to lose weight wisely. If you are vegetarian, make sure you eat a mix of vegetables, grains and beans so you take in the balanced proteins you would normally get from meats. Iron is found in green leafy vegetables, peppers, cabbage, tomatoes, meats and eggs.

Clogged Drains

If you make it halfway through war and peace before seeking any results in the bathroom (i.e. you are constipated) its time for you to add some **fiber** in your diet.

> As you increase your fiber, make sure you increase your fluid intake as well.

Solution

On an average you need 25-30 gms of fiber per day. Start your day right with a fruit and high fiber or any cereal breakfast (i.e. a bowl of cornflakes, oatmeal etc.), include chapattis and pulses (beans, chanas) for lunch, snack on roasted chana in the evening and include a large platter of salad in your dinner. Increase fiber gradually. If you were living on a diet of white bread and scrambled eggs till today, don't suddenly start on beans, chanas etc. Go slow and add one high fiber item at a time to your diet till your body gets used to it.

A Racing Heart

If you feel your heart suddenly racing or fluttering for no good reason, its alarming. If it is accompanied by any pain or dizziness, consult your doctor, right now. But what if your doctor says that nothing is wrong and your heart still keeps racing or changing its pace at random, you may be suffering from deficiency of **magnesium or potassium** in your diet.

Solution

Start your day with a glass of banana shake. A variety of leafy greens, pulses, beans and whole grains (wheat) during the rest of the day will ensure adequate intake of these trace minerals.

Frequent Memory Slip Ups

If you feel that you tend to forget things easily, loose your train of thoughts and stumble over your words, you are not taking enough **B vitamins**.

Solution

Think B for beans and breakfast cereals since they are healthiest source of B6 and folate. B12 is found in abundance in most meats and seafoods.

Sore Gums

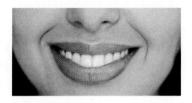

If you face the problem of sore gums quiet frequently then its time for you to include acidophilus bacterium in your diet. This beneficial bacterium helps in regulating the natural flora in your mouth and protects you from gum problems.

Solution

Have a cup of **yogurt** with lunch and dinner everyday.

> Walnuts too are an excellent source of Omega -3 fatty acids. A good food for the vegetarians!

Creaking Joints

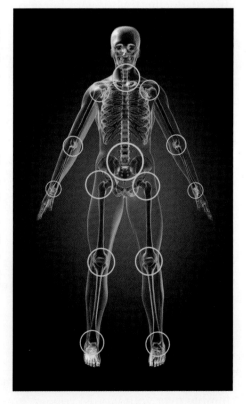

If you find all your joints aching, don't blame arthritis (in every case), blame a lack of fish in your food if you are a non-vegetarian.

Solution

Replace your chicken or mutton fry with a serving of fish twice a week for dinner. Mounting evidences suggest that **omega 3 fatty acids** found in fish like cod, sardine, mackerel etc. can help joints move more smoothly while increasing blood flow and reducing swelling and pain around joints.

FOLK REMEDIES

Countries throughout the world have their folk remedies based on natural food and herbs, which are mostly effective without any side ill effects. Common seasonings added to food can kill bacteria that cause food poisoning. Good bacteria-fighters are garlic and clove, followed by cinnamon, oregano and sage.

1. **Asthma:**

    (i) Concoction made by mixing 1 tbsp juice of bitter gourd (kerala) and 5-6 crushed leaves of *Tulsi (basil)* and sweetened with honey is a good expectorant.

    (ii) ½ tsp powdered safflower seeds mixed with 1 tbsp honey, also acts as a good effective expectorant.

2. **Constipation** is cured by plant-based medicine. Cassia senna and castor oil are used as laxatives.

3. **Cancer & Heart:** **Nuts** add taste and texture to a variety of dishes from sweets to salads, cereals to rich dishes, stir-fries. Besides that nuts are heart healthy, they contain phyto-chemicals, the plant substance that is thought to reduce the risk of diseases like cancer. Also nuts are cholesterol free and a great plant source of protein. They are rich in nutrients and fiber, are nutrition-dense snack, a hand full of **almonds**, one serving, have 160 calories, one ounce of almonds gives you beneficial amount of vitamin E, magnesium, calcium, also gives mono-unsaturated fat, potassium, phosphorous and iron. Peanuts are high in foliate and 1 oz of pistachios provide the same amount of potassium as half banana.

Thus nuts are a healthy snack:

Small quantity (a fist size or table tennis ball size, 1.5oz/1/3 cup) of nuts, daily, provides:

(i)   Healthful fats without creating obesity.

(ii) The nuts are also good for healthy hair. **Almonds and walnuts** are source of Omega-6 fatty acids.

    *   Take ¼ cup or 1½ handful of these nuts a day, which is the recommended serving by F.D.A. (U.S.A. Food & Drug Administration).

    *   To eat right, take a handful of plain assorted nuts instead of a couple of biscuits. Toss some stir-fried nuts to your salad or pasta.

    *   Sprinkle chopped nuts into breakfast cereal, soup or vegetables.

    *   Spread a single layer of whole, chopped or sliced nuts on a non-greased baking pan. Bake them at 180°C for about 10 minutes or until light brown. Cool and eat as a snack.

4. ***Pancreatitis - Inflammation of the Pancreas*** – the folk remedy of Philippines, Filipino folk healers, treat the patient suffering from this, by administrating the fresh juice of guava, papaya or mango, and this gives excellent results.

    Drinking small amount of fruit juices like juice of pears, apple, guava, mango and papaya are neutral juices and will cure upset disturbed stomach.

5. ***Peptic ulcer caused*** by H. pylori is a **serious gut problem**. Folk remedy for this is: Put 5 drops of tea-tree oil in a glass of diluted milk, drink this twice daily with meals. It gives relief to pain and kills bacteria.

6. ***Food Poisoning***, use herbs like powered slippery elm, fenugreek seeds, powered blackboard chalk, milk of magnesia, or activated charcoal (powdered or tablets). Any one of the above when taken mixed with a little milk works great for food poisoning.

7. ***Hungarian Grandmother's Folk Treatment for Palsy-Paralysis*** of the muscles on one side of the face, due to **inflammation of the facial nerves**, which run from a tiny hole in the bone between the ear and the jaw. The inflammation compresses the nerve inside its bony channel, **resulting in the paralyzing** of the muscles between the forehead and the mouth. People age between 30-60 i.e. older people seem to be the most susceptible.

Treatment by Tea: Lay warm compresses of chamomile or spear-mint tea upon the afflicted sides of the patient's face and then place a dry cloth over it to retain the heat longer. Change the compress every 7 minutes, and replace it with another hot one.

8. *Prostrate Cancer:* Fruits and vegetables that are crimson colored are of great benefit to the prostrate. The red ripe tomatoes on account of their cancer fighting lycopene are recommended for the patients. Other beneficial foods are cranberries, cranberry juice, strawberries, raspberries, currants, red grapes, radish, apples with their peels, beets, pink grape-fruit, red onions and water melon. Soya foods, though not of a reddish color, are of equal medicinal value for good prostrate health.

Benign Prostrate Hyperplasia - Enlargement of Prostrate: This is old age growing process, patient urinates with difficulty and has to go to the bath room frequently even at night. He cannot urinate freely, and relieve himself with much obvious strain.

Folk healing for this is a dietary approach, which gives a permanent solution.

Note: Men who took high- meat, high fat, high sugar diet and very little fruits and vegetables, or fiber, have greater risk of getting enlarged prostrate- as well as prostrate cancer.

Beneficial foods are **tomatoes** in any form, **nuts**, especially **hazelnuts or pecans** in small quantity, **seeds like pumpkin seeds** which are full of zinc, certain fibers (especially cooked **oatmeal and shredded wheat**), fruits such as **kiwi** (rich in vitamin E & K), mango and papaya, root vegetables such **as turnips, carrots and potatoes** (baked, boiled, steamed, juiced or raw), Dark leafy greens like- **parsley, endive, romaine lettuce and spinach**.

Within two months, you could see the relief in the prostrate problem, you can urinate in 1/3 the time and with less pain and effort.

9. *Skin Problems:*

(i) **Acne** can be remedied by richly colored leafy greens like spinach, fenugreek, drumstick leaves etc. These are full of anti oxidants, plus they are a great source of iron when eaten with vitamin C rich foods. Women who don't get enough iron are specially, prone to dark circles under their eyes. Greens also contain zinc. Tomato keeps skin elastic: Ripe tomato packs high levels of the antioxidant vitamins A and C as well as skin cancer fighting chemicals.

Vitamin C helps keep skin elastic and prevents bruising. Vitamin A aids in healing acne from the inside out by boosting resistance to infection.

(ii) **Defeat Dryness:** When the skin does not get sufficient good fats found in poly and monounsaturated oils like sesame, mustard, peanuts and olive in the diet, it becomes persistently dry, flaky skin. When good fats are added back in food, the condition usually clears up in a few weeks.

(iii) **Dehydrated skin** looks ashen and gray. Water makes the skin hydrated. Hydrated skin looks moist and plump, which makes existing wrinkles less obvious. Drink 9, 200ml glasses of water, daily. Berries are a great source of antioxidants that are helpful in fighting wrinkles. A handful of strawberries, or 2-3 gooseberry has all the antioxidant vitamin C your body requires each day to reconstruct your collagen.

(iv) **Wrinkles:** Melon is full of carotene-like compounds such as lycopene, which reduce the deep down collagen damage that promotes **wrinkles**. A slice of melon a day promotes a healthy glow.

10. *For Persistent Acne:* Rinse face and apply a mask of plain yogurt for 15-30 minutes. The lactic acid in yogurt is a natural exfoliate that gives skin a glow, clears acne, and fades de-colorations and fine lines.

11. *Mosquito Bite:* The swelling and itching caused by a mosquito bite can be reduced with aspirin paste. Aspirin contains salicylic acid, the active ingredient, which has medicinal properties. Crush a low dose aspirin tablet, add one oz water and dissolve it, then apply to the affected area. The anti-inflammatory properties of aspirin reduce the redness from bites or strings, pimples, and ingrown nails.

12. *Eczema and Psoriasis* flare-ups can be soothed by applying olive oil directly to the irritated area. Rub I tsp of olive oil to per square inch area, it creates a seal so skin won't dry out. Olive oil is the basis of many moisturizers but used alone, it lacks chemical irritants present in the moisturizing creams. For serious cases, cover oil- slathered skin with plastic wrap overnight. These rashes rarely turn into broken skin, but if they do, skip the home treatment and see a doctor immediately.

13. *To Minimize Scaring:* As the wound heals, keep the skin soft to minimize the scaring. I massaged with Vitamin E oil, on my head wound scar. The scar has nearly gone. You can also keep your scar moist with petroleum jelly and bandage for 3-5 days.

At night put cellophane tape over the jelly. Tape will keep the water trapped into the skin better than breathable bandage, encouraging healthy collagen growth.

14. ***Sprains - Salt and Vinegar Treatment:*** This is very effective for sprains. Heat one cup of water. Add to it 1 tbsp salt and ½ cup white vinegar. Soak a cloth in the mixture, wring it out, and wrap it around the sprained area. When the cloth begins to cool, soak it again in the hot mixture and reapply. Reheat the vinegar salt solution on low heat before applying again. This reduces the pain and swelling. Repeat this twice daily till the pain and swelling is completely gone.

15. ***Cuts & Wounds: For Internal Bleeding:*** Mix ¼ tsp powdered red pepper in 1 cup tomato juice and drink it. Bleeding should cease within minutes.

    Caution: For any kind of serious injury, always see a doctor before attempting self-treatment.

    Bleeding cuts, not very serious, can be washed with soap and water, disinfect them with apple cider vinegar. Minor bleeding wounds can be treated by applying cayenne pepper powder or turmeric powder liberally.

16. ***Open Wounds:*** Likewise sugar is an excellent disinfectant for open wounds or skin ulceration, sprinkle on granulated sugar to help kill bacteria and speed healing. Smear a ring of petroleum jelly around the edges of the wound to hold sugar in place, then put a little sugar directly on the wound. Cover the area with a bandage and be sure to change the bandage once or twice a day.

THE POWER OF
YOGA & EXERCISE

THERAPIES FOR SELF HEALING

YOGA BASICS

Indian Yoga Therapy

Yoga combines physical exercise, deep breathing methods (Pranayama) and Meditation, promoting balance between your mind, body and spirit. The philosophy of yoga teaches that optimal health requires a harmonious union between mind and body.

Yoga therapies tap your body's power to heal. You can explore the therapies suited for you and ways to take better care of yourself.

> **Yoga** means 'to join' or 'to unite'. The question is with whom? Yoga Gurus explain, Yoga is to establish **unity with the ultimate Reality -'God'.** The word 'Yoga' originates from the Sanskrit word 'Yuj' which means 'to center ones thoughts', 'to concentrate oneself or to meditate deeply'.

> **Yoga postures** help people lose weight, overcome fears, conquer habits like smoking, and develop better concentration, all of which help their performance in their daily tasks. Yoga includes **physical exercises** that relax and still the body, **breath work** to focus the mind, **relaxation** to calm the body and mind, **chanting** to arouse and then calm the emotions and **meditation** to center the spirit.

Never too old or overweight for Yoga...

You are never inflexible, overweight or too old for yoga's gentle technique. Gentle approach to yoga is ideal to increase flexibility, improve blood circulation, vitality and posture. When you learn to modify postures, you become safe and comfortable in your own body.

Precautions of Yoga Therapies

1. Patients should always consult their physician before starting any sort of activity.

2. Heart patients and those who have blood pressure should do simple mild exercises with least pressure on the heart and its beat, e.g. do pranayama slowly & with care. Start by doing ten times then slowly increase to 20 and then 30 times i.e. less than 30 seconds.

3. When your heart and lungs get stronger eventually doing the pranayama, you can slowly and very carefully increase the time of the exercise.

4. Rest: Listen to your body and rest, when you feel tired. Rest not only prevents injuries that come from overuse, but it also keeps you feeling fresh and inspired to stay active.

5. Warmed & Stretched Muscles: If the muscles are not sufficiently warmed up and stretched before doing yoga postures, they are susceptible to being strained. This can range from a small tear to a complete separation of the muscle from the tendon. A sprain occurs when a ligament, which connects bone to bone, is stretched too far. Backache is caused by repetitive strain, not just a single injury.

6. If suddenly your back starts to ache, stop the exercise and rest for a day, but do not stop for a long time.

   (i) Start your exercising routine again slowly and cautiously.

   (ii) Avoid bending unnecessarily, do not turn abruptly.

   (iii) Avoid carrying heavy loads (weights) as in gardening and shopping.

   (iv) Sit straight. If pain continues, take pain killer and start gentle stretching back exercises. Once your back pain is controlled, start back exercises in full to make back muscles strong.

7. Massage on the back with herbal oil will also help the pain. Plant essential oils assist in cell regeneration and healing when applied to the skin. But as these oils are concentrated they should be diluted with vegetable oils before applying to the skin. Direct application of concentrated essential oils results in skin irritation. Essential oils are almonds, sunflower, grape-seeds, or fresh kernel oil concentration of the essential oils. Any of these can be used for massaging.

EXERCISES FOR NATURAL HEALING

My workout plan is a combination of different comparative therapies. Starting with 15 minutes of workout, I slowly and gradually increased to one hour workout within 6 months. I will share with you the most beneficial exercises, yoga postures and comparative therapies that I have practiced in my daily routine that have helped me in handling numerous common ailments.

The combination of therapies includes therapeutic stretching, joint mobilization, soft tissue manipulation, rhythmic rocking, acupressure and energy balance with assisted Yoga postures. With this combined powerful tool you can direct your body's own vital force towards healing yourself on all levels - emotional, mental and physical. I started my workout, first thing in the morning after awakeing, with 'Wake up spine exercise'.

Wake Up Spine : Back Ache

This exercise is very effective immediately on awaking. It also helps remove backache. It gets your circulation going after a full night's sleep, and if you sleep on your stomach, especially, stretches out your vertebrae. It also gives relief to cramps by stretching the lower calves of legs.

Exercise

1. Lie on your back with your legs extended straight out in front of you, and your arms above your head straight.

2. Stretch your whole body. Imagine that you are making yourself tall. Hold for 10 seconds. Relax for 10 seconds.

3. Keeping the lower part of your body straight only bend and stretch your torso to the left, with your extended arms and shoulders. Hold for 10 seconds. Release and come to the original position.

4. Bend on the right side and stretch your torso extending your arms and shoulders. Hold for 10 seconds. Release and come to the original straight position.

After that to **warm myself up I do 5 minutes on the spot walking or jogging or marching on a point**, i.e. while standing, moving my legs up and down just like doing brisk walking, jogging or marching.

> Simple spot marching for 5 minutes helps cure constipation and gas formation

Neck Pain

Neck Pain could be due to: sitting for long in a car or at a desk; working on a computer; having poor posture; or a bad sleeping position; and reacting to stress and tension; all exert a great demand on the neck structure. As a result (i) some muscles can atrophy, (ii) tendons can shorten and (iii) ligaments can lose their tensile strength. The muscular pain can cause not only neck problems, but also headaches and radiating pain in the arms and shoulders.

Stiffness and pain can be temporarily released by massaging the shoulders and neck. Neck massage with herbal clove oil, gave me relief from neck pain.

I. Neck & Shoulder Exercise

(i) Sit in any asana preferably, Sukhasana (page 56). Bend your arms and put your hands over your shoulders, right hand over the right shoulder and left hand over the left shoulder.

(ii) Rotate your hands over their respective shoulders in a clock-wise direction for 10 rounds.

(iii) Then rotate in anti-clockwise direction for 10 rounds.

II. Neck Stretching and Strengthening Exercise

Interlock your fingers of both hands, and place them behind your neck. Now take a deep breath and try to press your neck backward and make your interlocked fingers push it in front. Do this gently and with just a little bit of strain. Breathe out and bring the neck to the original position with hands on the back. Repeat 10 times. Bring your hands down.

III. Upper and Lower-Back Stretch

Releases tension in the neck, arms, shoulder and lower back muscles, rotates the joints, also strengthens the neck and upper and lower back.

1. Put your hands at the back above the hip, palms facing outward & holding one hand with the other.

2. Keep your shoulder straight.

3. Take a deep breath push your shoulder to the back, breath out and bring the shoulders to their original positions, to the front. Repeat this 10 times.

IV. Arms, Shoulders & Hands Stretch

Strengthens and stretches the arms, shoulders and hands muscles.

1. Sit with crossed legs in an asana. Take your hands to the head and catch your wrists with your opposite hands in a lock. Take your locked hands behind your head.

2. Take a deep breath, and lower your joint arms on the right side of the head lowering the bent arms towards the right shoulder.

3. Try to pull the right hand with the left hand. Breathe out and bring your hands back over the head in the middle.

4. Take a deep breath and tilt your arms towards the left of the head. Lower the bent arms towards the shoulder. Pull the left arm with your right hand. Breathe out and return the locked hands in the middle of the head. This completes one round.

Cramps

Frequently, I used to have cramps, even while sleeping, it was really painful.
Cramps occur...

1. When muscles in the foot are **contracted** for an extended period of time.

2. When your **foot is pinned** in a bent position under a tight bed sheet or you are standing and suddenly this problem occurs. This can produce irritation of the nerves, muscles and tendons in your foot and calf and shooting pain is felt in the calf of the leg.

3. When you are **pointing your toes** while swimming or dancing.

4. Cramps also normally **signal dehydration** or **an over worked muscle**.

5. When, you exercise, you can also develop cramp **from heavy sweating**, which depletes your body of the mineral needed to maintain proper muscle function.

6. In **pregnancy and in old age** too, the cramps are common.

7. May be due to **weakness** or some **nutrient deficiency**.

Stretches and Massage to Cure Cramps

It used to take me 5-10 minutes to massage the effected muscle to release the nerve to stop the pain. Even then that muscle remained slightly sore throughout the day.

1. **Take lots of water** throughout the day, to keep yourself hydrated, if the cramps are brought by vigorous exercise.

2. **Stretching your foot while massaging** will usually relieve this discomfort.

3. Stretch your calves, by simply lifting yourself up on your toes, reach out with your arms, elongating your entire spine. Hold for 5 counts and repeat twice more.

Comparative Remedies

An ice pack will help the cramps disappear.

Sleeping Hands, Fingers & Toes

This exercise strengthens and circulates the blood in the legs, feet, toes and ankles. Also helps sleeping feet.

Foot, Toes & Ankle exercise

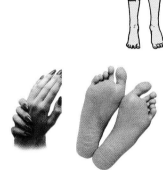

1. Sit with the legs extended straight in front, with feet joined and facing up. Put your hands at the back just behind your shoulders, touching the ground. Also push your shoulders a little to the back.

2. Rotate your feet in clockwise direction 10 times. Then rotate them in anticlockwise direction 10 times.

3. Sit in the initial position. Now move the toes of both feet up and down in a rhythmic position. Do 10 times. Relax.

Interesting Exercises for the Feet

a. Simply walking bare foot on sand is a good way to make lazy toes grip and flex themselves. Try picking up pebbles with your toes.

b. Sit on a chair, with one leg crossed the other near the knee. Rotate the foot, which is off the floor in a clockwise direction, working from the ankle. Keep rotating it in one direction for 30 seconds, then in the other direction for 30 seconds. Then change the sitting position and work with the other foot repeating the same movements.

Teeth

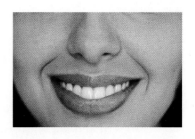

My teeth too are not giving me any trouble now! Earlier I had great pain in one tooth and another tooth was loose. The dentist in America advised me wrongly, to take out the tooth that was loose and to get root canal done to the other. I was not convinced with the doctor, so I did not get the treatment done in America. I came to India and got opinions of two dentists in India, they both told me that root canal was out of question as my jaw bone had reduced due to age and I should take both of the teeth out. I refused to get them extracted. I **massaged my gums with gum-paint** twice daily for a month. I was astonished to note that my pain had completely gone and the loose tooth stopped giving me trouble. I now do not feel as if there is a loose tooth at all, as I do not feel any difficulty in eating, even whole nuts like almonds. I also tried my natural ways of brushing my teeth with herbal tooth paste (*neem*). Also, doing the Shitkari Pranayama helped me a lot.

Shitkari Pranayama, which is for teeth, pyorrhea etc.

1. Sit in any asana. Touch your tongue to your palate closely.

2. Close both your jaws with the upper and lower teeth joining closely. Keep the lips open.

3. Breathe in through the mouth passing in the air between the teeth through the closed jaws. Fill the lungs to their full capacity.

4. Retain the air in as long as you can. (Can skip this).

5. Now close the mouth and breathe out slowly through the nose releasing the bandha.

Repeat the exercise as many times as you can. But this should not be done repeatedly in cold weather.

Benefits:

(i)   Cures diseases relating to teeth, pyorrhea etc. and diseases of throat cavity, mouth, nose, tongue.

(ii) Beneficial in the diseases relating to throat and spleen etc. Cures indigestion. Helps to control thirst & hunger. Lowers high blood pressure. Purifies blood.

(iii) Helps cure sleepiness, makes the blood cool.

(iv) If done regularly 50-60 times daily for long period can cure hypertension.

Hair Falling

Hair falling has stopped and while combing my hair, they do not break as they used to before. This is the effect of yoga and herbal oil massage. My hair has also become smooth and I feel my hair has become a little thicker too.

Increasing of grey hair has also stopped. For this I rub my 8 nails of both hands with each other for 5 minutes daily. The rubbing of nails is associated with the hair, on doing this the hair remains black for a long time.

Rubbing Nails Exercise:

1. Sit in an asana, bend your arms in front, so that your hands are in front of the chest.

2. Half close your wrists, bring your 8 nails of both hands opposite facing one another, now rub the nails with each other for 30 seconds.

Eyes

During my routine check up of my eyes, I was happy to note that my eyesight number had not increased, which shows that my **'Eye and Neck Exercises'** had steadied my eye- sight. It also removed the haziness and tiredness of my eyes.

Eye & Neck Exercise

1. Stand straight. Take a deep breath and twist your head to the right as far as possible as if your ear is touching your shoulder. Look to the right as far as you can. Hold for 10 seconds.

2. Exhale and bring back your head in its original position i.e. in front.

3. Now turn your head towards left and repeat the above two steps, while moving your eyes towards the left. Hold for 10 seconds. Breathe out and bring your head to the original position.

4. Raise your head while breathing in, bend it upwards towards the ceiling as far as possible, while looking towards the ceiling. Hold for 10 seconds. Breathe out and bring your head to the original position.

5. Breathe in and bend your head and eyes towards the chest, touching your chin to the depression in the neck. Look at your nose. Hold for 10 seconds. Breathe out and bring your head up to the original position.

6. Rotate your head in clock wise direction, rotating your eyes with it. Repeat 10 times.

7. Now rotate your head and eyes in anti-clock wise direction. Repeat 10 times.

8. Rub palms together vigorously for a few seconds. Close your eyes and cover eyes with the palms. Take five very slow deep breaths, visualizing new energy and brightness into the eyes. Gently massage your eyes.

Benefits: Relieves headache and eye strain; improves eye sight. It relaxes neck and shoulder tensions.

ALL ABOUT BREATHING

Breathing is automatic and you don't think about it. But, actually you should give attention to breathing especially while working-out (exercising).

Effectiveness of an exercise program, at any level, depends on the impact by breathing efficiency and technique. Besides food and water, your body needs to process oxygen, transferring it from the lungs, through the blood-stream to the muscles.

Breathing is an integral part of any exercise. Weight lifters and body builders exhale so forcefully while they are lifting that they make a sound. Even ordinary people are instructed to 'breathe on the exertion' when they are on weight-training programs. Lamaze and other child-birth preparation programs use controlled breathing as a way to relax. In ordinary breathing, a person daily takes 20,000 breaths, most of which are shallow inhalations in which air does not reach deep into the lungs. Shallow breathing tightens neck muscles, which in turn can cause stiffness and pain.

> Deep breathing can supply air to each lung cell thus cleaning the impurities of blood and rendering it pure, the impure air is then thrown out. If the lungs become somewhat diseased, the breathing slows down resulting in slow heart beat. This reduces the purification of blood and impure blood starts circulating in the body, resulting in skin rashes, eczema etc.

Proper Breathing

Breathing should not be shallow chest breathing in which only rib cage rises and falls. The proper breathing promotes **a breathing form that is rhythmic and engages the abdominal and diaphragm muscles** to breathe deeply and properly. Massage of the connective tissues in the chest, back, arms and abdomen loosens the muscles and facilitates unrestricted breathing. Breathing properly is relaxing and stress-reducing, and it is less taxing on your performance as well as giving a push to your body's metabolism.

With proper breath therapy, you can relearn proper breathing techniques, which will help to remove asthma and insomnia, increase metabolic rate and improve your immune system.

PRANAYAMA AND ASANAS
Understanding in Depth

Pranayama

Prana is air or breath. Breathing in air deeply and breathing out of air is called Pranayama. Daily pranayama on empty stomach gives you best benefits for health and makes you less susceptible to diseases.

In terms of yoga, the air which you take in is called 'Poorak' and complete holding of air is called 'Kumbuk'. Breathing out of the air is called 'Raychak' and when you hold air out, it is called 'Brahm Kumbak'. Holding of breath increases mental faculties, making you more alert mentally.

Taking in of the air is inspiration and taking out of the air is expiration. Normally we do not breathe deeply to full capacity and only ¼ of the breathing process is done by us in our normal life activity. Like a bees hive, our lungs have 73 million air pockets of which only 20 million openings get the air with our light breathing, the rest of the 43 million openings remain functionless. As a result the unused openings get blocked with waste, giving rise to T.B. (tuberculosis), cough, bronchitis etc. Blood is not purified completely by normal breathing. Always breathe through your nose, as clean air enters the lungs after being filtered in the nose.

When I started regular Pranayama my **blood pressure** became normal and I lost weight about 15-16 lbs. My tummy reduced and now it does not hang over the waist belt as it used to. All this is due to breathing exercises.

How to do Pranayama?

1. Pranayama should be done in the morning, after nature's call. Pranayama should always be done at least 4-5 hours after meals on an empty stomach.

2. Your mind should be calm, peaceful and devoid of any worries in the morning while doing the Pranayama.

3. Keep your eyes closed throughout the exercise, as it needs concentration.

4. If you feel tired while doing a pranayama take 5-6 long breathes and a short rest before starting second pranayama.

5. Pregnant women and those who are unwell and have fever should not do pranayama.

6. Pranayama should be done slowly, without haste, patiently & with care.

7. Doing pranayama you should increase the speed and time with patience. Remember you should not increase the time and speed at the same time in the same pranayama.

8. Doing any pranayama, if you feel even a slightest pain in the left part of your chest, it is a sign of over exertion and that you have done more than your body is capable of doing. In such a case stop the exercise immediately and rest for some days before starting again.

9. While practicing pranayama head, neck, shoulders and back should be straight while sitting. Only then it will be done in the right way and will be beneficial.

10. Do not hold your breathe with force. Do it with ease as long or as short as you can.

Pranayama and Age

Deep breathing and age have a great relation with each other, this phenomena is the main pillar on which Indian culture is based. According to Indian Philosophy, our life span is fixed and measured in the total number of breaths you take. So,

1. One who increases the time between inhaling and exhaling by pranayama will increase his or her age, accordingly.

2. It is also said that the person who does regular pranayama, cleanses oneself internally and enlightens with knowledge. The knowledge thus attained continues to increase till death.

3. The first step in Pranayama is to learn to tune into the rhythm of the breath and regulate it. A smooth, slow rhythm usually indicates a relaxed state of body and mind. Worries are removed with solutions when you do pranayama, your body, mind, thought and soul are purified.

Asanas

A Yoga Asana is a posture where you are externally still yet internally alive. The Pranayama is done by sitting in one of the following different Asanas.

1. **Asana:** To sit normally with folded legs, feet on your opposite side on the ground.

2. **Sukhasana**, in this put your left foot on the ground under the right leg and the right leg folded over the left fore leg.

3. **Padhasana:** This is also known full lotus Asana. When in Asana both legs are folded & both feet are taken upon the opposite thighs near the knees.

4. **Varjasana:** Sit with both legs bent behind on the back; slowly put your hips on the joined feet at the back. Sit like this till you are at ease in the asana. If you feel any strain or pressure on the legs, stop the asana and relax and sit straight.

   When you have practiced this asana regularly your body will get adjusted to it and you can sit in this asana for some time.

5. **Manduk Asana:**

   (i) Sit in Varjasana. Breathe in and breathe out, press your stomach with joint fists with the thumbs side.

   (ii) Bend forward to touch the head to the ground. Breathe in slowly. Raise your head and upper body to straight sitting position.

   (iii) Repeat this 2-3 times. Come back to Varjasana.

Benefits: Good for gas, sinuous, digestive system.

Pawanmukta Asana

This exercise removes gas and other stomach ailments.

1. Lie straight on your back and try to touch your left knee to your chest.

2. Interlock the fingers of both hands and put them on the left knee. Press your knee to your chest and raise your head and try to touch your nose to the left knee. Hold this position for 10-30 seconds. Then bring your leg down and lie straight. Repeat this 2-4 times.

3. Repeat these movements with the right leg and right knee.

4. Then do with both the knees, raising the knees to the chest and touch your nose to the knees. Hold for 10-30 seconds.

5. Then bring your head and knees down on the floor and lie straight relaxed. This completes one round. Repeat 3-4 times to practice.

Benefits:

*   Helps digest your food without the formation of gas.

*   This asana is beneficial for pregnant women.

*   Heart diseases and arthritis pains are also controlled by this asana.

*   Belly fat is reduced.

Precautions: Those with pain in the waist or back- ache should not raise their head to touch the knee. They should only touch the knees to the chest. This will benefit slip disc, sciatica or back ache.

Types of Pranayama

While doing breathing exercises you should be stress free, happy and peaceful. Do not think about your work, home or other things that you have planned for the day. Just focus fully on the breathing.

Breathing in yoga is divided into three areas:

1. Low (tummy or diaphragm):
2. Middle (chest or thoracic):
3. Upper (upper chest or clavicular):

Some of the Most Important Pranayama are

Bhastrika Pranayama

This is the very first pranayama.

1. Sit crossed legs in Sukhasana (page 56) i.e. sit normally crossed legs on the floor with ease. Those who cannot sit on floor they can sit on a chair. But it is very important that while doing this asana, your backbone i.e. your back should be straight.

   Note: Some people have started doing pranayama while walking when they go to morning or evening walks. This can do harm instead of giving you benefits. Pranayama is always done sitting with a straight back.

2. Take a deep breath (inhale) with all your might, by both your nostrils in a rhythmic count of 10 beats.
3. Hold the breath for a rhythmic count of 5.
4. Then take out the breath (exhale) with full force during the count of 10.

Repeat this procedure of inhaling and exhaling three times, according to one's capacity, as it should be done with ease.

Healthy people or those who are already doing breathe in and breathe out Pranayama can increase the speed of this exercise. You can do this pranayama, in three speeds - slow, medium and high.

Precautions:

1. Start this paranayama in slow speed, then, slowly increase to medium and ultimately to high.

2. Patients with high blood pressure, heart disease and weak lungs, should not do this pranayama with high speed, they should do only slowly.

3. When doing the pranayam you breathe in, do not expand the stomach, the breath should be taken in up-to the diaphragm which will expand the lungs and chest only.

4. While breathing out, take the breath out with as much force as you can.

5. This exercise should be done for limited time during hot climate.

6. In case you have a cold or sinus problem, when you cannot open both your nostrils, you should do the breathing in and out at whatever speed you can. You first close your right nostril, and with the left nostril, breathe in and out at whatever speed you can. Then close the left nostril and breathe in and out with your right nostril at slow, medium, or quick speed. Then in the end try with both the nostrils.

Do this exercise regularly for 3-5 minutes, daily. This will help in opening your nostrils.

Benefits:

*   Cold, running nose, allergies, breathing difficulty, sinus, etc. are cured by this exercise.

*   Ailments like thyroid, tonsils, any defect in the throat are treated with it.

*   Pure air, which enters the lungs, keeps heart and lungs healthy.

*   The blood is purified.

*   It increases the immunity and keeps your mind calm and peaceful.

Kapalbharti Pranayam

This exercise differs a little from Bhastrika pranayama, where breathe in and breathe out are done with equal force, whereas in Kapalbharti breathe out is done with force while breathe in is done normally.

> Kapal means forehead; Bharti stands for light, enlightment. This pranayama brightens your forehead, and light shines from your face, say the pranayama Gurus.

Breathe in (inhale) normally but breathe out (exhale) with force and concentration to throw out the impure air completely. Doing this your stomach goes in and out automatically in a rhythmic order. To do kapalbharti pranayam...

1. Sit in Sukhasana (page 56) and now with full force breathe out.

2. Repeat this pranayama, breathe out for at least 30 times.

3. Do the exercise slowly, at first. Gradually increase the speed and the time duration - from 1 minute to 3 to 5 minutes.

Note:

1. Do not over exert yourself. At the start you will be tired after 1 minute.

2. Just relax and rest. Then begin again.

3. This exercise should be done regularly at least for 3 minutes. After two months of regular practice you will be able to do this pranayama for 5 minutes with ease.

4. Initially, you may get a little backache, which will go automatically in time.

5. In hot weather you should practice this only for 2 minutes.

Doing this pranayama you should think that with the breath you throw out, you are taking out all the ailments of your body. Thinking enhances the benefits of the pranayama.

Caution: High blood pressure and heart patients should start the pranayama slowly.

Benefits: Has beneficial effects on diseases like obesity, menstruation, gas and constipation. Is also benefits kidney and prostrate ailments.

* Cures cough, asthma, breathing, allergies, sinus etc.

* Good for all heart, lungs, and head ailments.

* Constipation is the root cause of all diseases and it can be cured by doing this pranayama regularly for 5 minutes, daily.

* It regularizes blood flow during menstruation, without taking any medicine.

* Removes obesity by reducing weight.

* Opens up the blockage in the heart.

* Removes depression by changing your attitude to optimistic, keeping you away from unpleasant thoughts, which result in calmness, stability and happiness.

* No other exercise has such beneficial effects on weak intestines by making them strong, and is very good for all stomach diseases.

* Also, removes pancreatic and urinary problems.

Anuloma-Viloma Pranayama (Alternate Nose Breathing)

In this pranayama the flow of your breath is directed by closing your nostrils alternatively. The pranayama should be started with the left nostril, as it is a sign of peace.

1. Open your right hand and place your right thumb lightly on your right nostril.

2. Keeping the palm of your hand a little above the nostrils, close the right nostril with the thumb. With your left nostril take a deep breath in a rhythmic count of 8 beats.

3. Keeping right nostril closed, close the left nostril with the middle finger. Both nostrils thus closed, hold the breath for a rhythmic count of 4.

4. Now remove your thumb from your right nostril and keeping the left nostril closed, slowly and deeply breathe out fully through the right nostril in a rhythmic count of 8.

5. When you have completely exhaled the air from your lungs with all your strength, resume inhaling this time with your right nostril (the same nostril through which you just finished exhaling).

> All vessels get purified with this asana. With the purification of all the body vessels the body becomes strong to fight ailments.

6. When the inhaling is completed, retain the air by closing both nostrils as before during a rhythmic count of 4. Without missing a beat, open your left nostril by removing the fingers and exhale deeply through the left nostril as before with the right nostril closed, when the breathing is complete, close your left nostril and simultaneously try to squeeze your anal muscles. Then breathe out completely from your right nostril with force.

Benefits:

* With squeezing of anal muscles during auloma-viloma, (step 6) your urinary bladder will benefit, the muscles of that region become strong. The saints called this awaking of the urinary organs as 'Kundali Jaggran', adopted by western doctors as Kegel Exercises for urinary incontinence, leakage of the bladder at the age of 50 and above.

* When doing this pranayama you keep meditating on 'OM'. This will take you to high yoga meditation, as if some light has entered in you.

* A number of diseases are cured by this pranayam, like heart disease, diabetes, urinary problems, cold, cough, asthma, sinus, chronic cold, arthritis, tonsils, general weakness, high blood pressure etc.

* Regular daily practice of this pranayama clears 30% to 40% of the blockages in 3 months. Cures cholesterol problems.

* Removes stress, in short it benefits you mentally, physically and spiritually. Purifies your thoughts and cures a number of diseases.

Bhramari Pranayama (Buzzing Bee Sound)

Humming bee breath sound seems to fill the skull like buzzing bee. The sound provides a point of focus for the mind.

1. Sit in Sukhasana (page 56), and take a deep breath to fill your lungs to the full.

2. Put your thumbs on both your ears to close them. Place the middle fingers of both hands on respective eyes to close them with little pressure.

3. Press forehead with both the forefingers lightly. Close your eyes then press eyes and the sides of the nose bridge with the remaining fingers.

4. Take a deep- breath and uttering 'Om' sound with your mouth closed.

5. Begin to take out your breath very slowly while making buzzing sound of a bee with mental recitation.

6. When the process of exhalation is complete the sound will stop for sometime.

7. Repeat the exercise 11 to 21 times according to your capacity. But start with 5 repetitions.

Benefits: This is great for meditation and concentration. Also cures throat diseases.

Murchha Pranayama

1. Sit in any asana, and close your eyes. Push your head a little backwards and look towards the roof. Through the nose breathe in. Retain breath.

2. Hold in this position as long as you can. Breathe out slowly and simultaneously close your eyes and bring your head to the original position in front.

3. Repeat these steps without break in between. Repeat 5 times. Do regularly.

Benefits: This is great for headache, eye-sight and memory.

Shayan-Paschimottanasana

1. Lie on your back with your legs straight. Join the heels and feet. Stretch your arms over your head straight.

2. While breathing out raise your body above the waist very slowly and bend over the feet and touch the toes with your hands. Hold for 2 seconds. Breathe in & slowly come back to the original position. Repeat 5-7 times.

Benefits: This is good for reducing fat from the stomach (belly fat) and keeping the digestive system fit.

Kevali Pranayama

1. Sit in a comfortable position. Inhale by both the nostrils slowly with mental recitation of "AUM", then exhale.

2. While inhaling, your concentration should be on the letter 'AU' and while exhaling concentration should be on the letter 'M' Thus one breath (in and out) will be completed with the mental recital of the mantra 'AUM'. Inhalation and exhalation are necessary to do mental recitation of AUM because meditation and pranayama are closely interlinked.

Benefits: Kevali Pranayama helps in improving the concentration of mind (dhyana).

> Making sounds is a great way to bring constancy to the breath. It also lengthens the exhalation which eventually deepens the inhalation and encourages a slow rhythmic breath.

MUDRAS AND BANDHAS

MUDRAS

Pranayama done with finger locks (mudras) give additional health benefit.

1. **Meditation Mudra:** Thumb represents Fire or Sun and Index finger represents Wind or Air.

   This mudra is formed when one touches the thumb with index finger. This interlocking of fingers increase brain-power, mental concentration, memory etc. thus cures sleeplessness.

2. **Vayu Mudra:** The index finger is kept at the base of the thumb at the mount of Varun, pressed with the thumb. Cures rheumatism, arthritis, gout, Parkinson's disease and blood circulation problems.

3. **Pran Mudra:** Here press the ring finger and little finger at the tip of the thumb. This is beneficial for the diseases which are cured by Vayu Mudra. This mudra gives better results also it increase life force and cures nervousness and fatigue. Helps increase power of the eyes and reduce the number of glasses.

4. **Shunya Mudra:** Bend your middle finger at the mount of venus and press it with the thumb. With the combination of these fingers, the mudras thus formed can control the five basic elements of which the body is formed. Do this 40 to 60 minutes to get best results. This helps to cure earache, deafness, vertigo etc.

5. **Prithvi Mudra:** Touch ring finger with your thumb. Gives new vigor and peace of mind. It increases life force, cures weakness of the body and mind.

6. **Varun (Water) Mudra:** Place the tip of thumb and little finger together as shown in Figure. Cures impurities of the blood, skin problems and makes skin smooth. Benefits gastro-enteritis and other disease causing dehydration

7. **Sun Mudra:** Bend the ring finger on to the palm and press the second fold with the thumb. This helps digestion, increase heat in the body and reduce fat of the body.

8. **Shiv Mudra:** Join both palms and interlock the fingers. Keep the left hand vertically straight and encircle it with the index finger and the thumb of the right hand.

9. **Bhajarava Mudra:** Sit in sidhasana, and do this mudra. In this rest your right hand on your left. Rest your hands in your lap, with your palms facing up and let the tips of the thumbs touch.

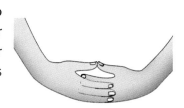

   This mudra increases both resistance against cold, changes in weather and also against bronchial infection, fever due to cold. It makes lungs create heat in the body and burn up accumulated phlegm and fat.

BANDHAS

If the mudra involves contraction of the muscles, it becomes a bandh.

Pranayama & Bandhas: Pranayama with Asanas and Bandhas prevent the vital energy flowing out of the body and preserves it inside. The Bandhas are very important in pranayama, as it is incomplete without Bandhas.

Bandh means 'to prevent' 'to tie' or to lock. It involves the contraction of certain muscles to unlock the pranic vital energies. The bandhas are very useful during asana practice. i) They work with the organs, the nervous and endocrine systems. ii). Can improve disorders of the reproductive and urinary systems, sexual dysfunction, back problems, iii) are also helpful after childbirth.

The three Bandhas, which are useful in Pranayama are:

1. *Jalandhara Bandha:*

   (i)   Sit in any yogic asana like Padmasana or Sukhasana (page 56). Inhale the air. While doing this, put both your palms on your knees.

   (ii)   Now bring your chin slowly down by lowering your neck and touching the chin to the pit in your neck.

   (iii)   Keep looking straight in the middle between your brows. Your chest will project itself forward.

   (iv)   Hold, then breathe out, and relax.

Benefits:

   (i)   This bandha has the effect of keeping together the nerves of the neck.

   (ii)   The voice becomes pleasant and charming.

   (iii)   All diseases of the neck & throat are cured, such as Thyroid, Tonsillitis etc.

2. *Uddiyana Bandha:*

   (i)   Stand on your feet slightly apart. Bend in front and keep your palms on your knees. I started with standing then continued by sitting in any of the yogi asanas for doing this bandha.

   (ii)   Breathe out and release the muscles of your stomach.

(iii)   Stretch your chest a little upward and try to push the stomach inside.

(vi)   Keep in this position as long as you can. Then breathe in and relax. Repeat after some rest. Do this bandha three times in the beginning then increase the number of times while doing regularly over the period of time.

Benefits:

(i)   When done regularly can cures diseases of the stomach and the organs of the digestive system.

(ii)   It also reduces belly.

3.   Moola Bandha:

(i)   Sit in Padamasana or Sukhasana (page 56). Breathe in and hold.

(ii)   Raise and contract the perineum part of the body i.e. the part between anus and genital organ, up. While doing so, the stomach region will be stretched up.

(iii)   This Bandha can be done with ease and convenience, by exhaling and holding out the air. Yogis, who are experienced in Yogic poses, can remain in this posture for several hours.

MORE YOGA ASANAS
from Animal Postures

Yoga is a way of life dating back 6,000 years. At first meditation was done in sitting asanas. Later ancient saints by studying animals found that the natural stretches of animals gifted by God give their bodies great health and strength benefits. When cats wake up they always stretch out beautifully. They reach forward and stretch back just like a yoga pose of Down-Facing Dog. Then they round their backs while arching up as yoga Cat Pose, and yawn.

Matsyasana - Fish Posture

1. Lie on your back. Raise the body on the arms and elbows. Let the head slowly fall backwards.

2. Raise the chest, arch the back and as you slide the elbows back down, rest the top of the skull on the floor. Put the weight on the head and buttocks.

3. Relax with arms beside the body and palms facing up, releasing all facial, neck and shoulder tensions.

4. Breathe deeply and slowly from the abdomen. Place the elbows beside the body as before to bear the weight, lift your head slowly. Hold the pose for 30 seconds or more with ease. Slide down into a lying position, while breathing out. Relax.

Benefits:

* Relieves constipation, bronchitis, asthma.

* Corrects posture defects; alleviates stiffness in spine, stimulates thyroid and parathyroid glands.

* Relaxes the neck and beautifies the neckline.

Giraffe Pose:

This is a front bending posture.

1. Stand straight, breathe in and bring your arms high above your head.

2. Breathe out, bend your body forward and put the hands on the floor as far as possible, keep the heels on the floor, stretch the back, looking down towards the rib cage.

Giraffe Pose

3. Walk on all fours moving right hand with right leg and left hand with left leg for 2 minutes. Breathe freely.

Benefits:

* The giraffe posture is useful for stomach and back muscles.

* It also strengthens the arms and legs.

Ustrasana - Camel Pose:

This pose is backward bend, strongly stretches the thighs, opens the groin and lifts the heart. The 5th chakra at the throat is activated in this posture where the head is tilted backward.

1. Kneel with your knees and hips wide apart. Tuck your toes under. Lift your right hand up and stretch in the air and bring the left hand down on the back and hold the heel, without twisting the body. Keep both hip and front ribs facing front. Take 5 breaths. Repeat on the other side. You get a feeling of lift as you extend back. This is to warm up for the full Ustrasana.

Camel Pose

2. While kneeling take both hands to the small of your back and massage it a little. The energy moves from the back of the waist to the ground through the knees. Maintain the lift through the spine from the back of the waist upward to open the chest. Take back the hands one by one to the heels. Stretch the hips forward and aim to have your thigh bones vertical. While rolling your shoulders back lift your breastbone to the sky. Now take your head back. Press your feet on the ground, inhale and come up. Repeat twice more.

Benefits: Thighs, groin and lifts heart.

Butterfly Leg Exercise:

Sit on the floor with bended legs, the feet joining, the under surface of both feet facing each other, in front of your body. Hold your feet with your hands. Move your bended legs up and down, like fluttering of butterfly wings. Continue this movement of the legs for 10 seconds.

Benefits: This strengthens and stretches the legs specially the thigh muscles.

Cat Stretch

1. Sit on the edge of a chair with your hands on your knees.

2. Exhale, slowly rounding your back and dropping your head between your knees.

3. Inhale, slowly lifting your head up and arching your back.

Benefits: Stretches your whole back.

Biralasana - Tiger Posture

It may not feel restful at first but it can become so when you develop strength and flexibility. To open the shoulders gently, hold and breathe in this pose longer. If you have wrist problems, begin with easier version.

1. Kneel down on your fours, with your hands about 6" in front of the shoulders, middle finger pointing straight ahead, and spread the fingers wide.

2. Keep the knees and feet apart. Tuck the toes under, lift up the back to an inverted 'V' position on tip toes, bend both knees deeply, so your ribs come toward the thighs, or even touch them.

3. You will feel an increase in the stretch through the shoulders and an opening in the chest. At the same time lift the hip as the buttocks stay high and tilt the pelvis forward.

The inward curve in the lower back will deepen as your naval moves closer to your thighs. You will feel the muscles along the spine working strongly and get a lifting sense of elongation along the spine.

4. Keeping the hip at the same height slowly straighten the legs. If the hip stays or nearly at, the same height everything in between will need to lengthen. Practice this several times, with full awareness, so you don't lose the feeling of height or the inward curve in the lower back.

Benefits: Tiger pose is probably the most widely used posture in hospitals in India as it helps straighten the spine, drains the sinuses, rests the heart, and improves breathing and circulation. Since you feel the strength and power of the tiger as you extend the spine, the name tiger is given to the pose.

Lion Posture: (Shing Asana)

1. Sit on your heels with knees slightly apart. Place palms on your knees, stiffly fan out your fingers.

2. Lean slightly forward.

3. Protrude the tongue as far as possible, contract the throat muscles, and roll the eye balls upwards, looking at the eye brow centre.

4. Completely exhale saying "Ahhhhhhh". Repeat 6 times.

Benefits:

1. Help relieve sore throat.

2. It stimulates circulation to throat and to tongue.

Downward Facing Dog Pose

1 Kneel on the floor. Place your hands far forward and lower your forehead to the floor.

2 Keep your knees under your hips so your buttocks are high in the air, not near the heels.

3. From the back of the waist, extend back strongly through the tailbone, at the same time direct your energy from the waist forward through the arms.

Benefits:

* This exercise brings awareness and flexibility to the entire length of the spine. The secret of awareness is to move slowly.

* It helps straighten the spine, cures sinuses; benefits the heart, as it improves breathing and circulation.

* In this posture all body organs come in the right position. This gives shoulders a good stretch.

Bhujangasana - Cobra posture:

Yoga for a flat tummy.

1. Lie on your stomach join your feet and stretch your legs straight. Keep your palms near the chest, elbows bent.

2. Slowly raise head, neck and chest, then your tummy, keeping your toes, feet and lower part of the body on the floor.

3. Stretch, neck slowly, and raise the head backwards as far as possible. Keep your eyes fixed to the ceiling or sky. The exercise will be complete when head, neck, chest and the upper part of the waist are high and you feel lots of pressure on the lower back & the waist joint.

4. At this point hold breath for 2-3 seconds. But, if you can't hold the breath, breathe normally, holding the pose for 20 seconds.

5. Now put your chest first on the floor then touch with your forehead and touching the floor with your left cheek let your body loose. Repeat this exercise 3 times.

Note:

* In the beginning one should not try to rise to the extreme position. One should go only as far as is comfortable and hold that position for the count of 10.

* Also, while doing this pose initially, you can use your palms as support but subsequently when you have practiced this exercise, you can put your palms on the floor and do the stretch without the help of the palms.

* Also when you have mastered the exercise you can breathe in while you raise your head and breathe out when you lower your head.

Benefits:

* While performing Cobra, you may be separating vertebrae that may be pushing upon one another, have strengthening effect upon the discs and entire back. For full benefits of the cobra, the spine must be continually arch.

* The arching relieves the tension.

* Within the period of about 2 weeks from the time you begin you should be able to attain the extreme position without strain. This will increase the flexibility of the spine, strengthen the arms and hands and open the throat (good for sore throat).

* The tilted head movement in this exercise helps to make certain that the neck muscles and the cervical vertebrae are brought into play.

* This asana keeps dorsal spine elastic and strong. It also reduces abdominal fat.

* It helps post-menopausal women to get rid of the intra-abdominal fat and in the process reduce their risk for some chronic diseases.

* This exercise can be done by everybody - men, women, young, old, and even patients.

Precaution: But pregnant women and those who have piles or hernia should not do this.

Whale Pose

Whale Pose is derived from Back push-up or Pelvic Raise.

1. Lie down with bent knees, joining the knees and the feet. Keep the knees up and arms at the sides.

2. Breathe in, as you breathe out make a sound of 'assss', raise the back from the floor. Hold and take 3 breaths, then breathe in and return to the floor. Imagine a whale coming to the surface of the ocean pushing upwards towards the ceiling and spreading a great spray. Repeat 3 times.

3. Rest by curling knees towards the chest and touching it.

Benefits:

* This posture strengthens the back and works the leg muscles.

* The breathing helps clear the lungs.

Alligator Posture

Benefits: Helps the stomach and back muscles and maintains posture.

The pose that alligators make while lumbering across the mud flats.

1. Lie on your stomach face down, hands to chest level and elbows close to your body, both feet joined.

2. Raise your head, breathe in and raise your head and both feet a little way off the floor.

3. Breathe out, breathing normally, push your body forward on your stomach, using your hands and swaying legs gently from side to side. Imitating the Alligator movement on the mud.

Mermaid Posture: Side Bend

Benefits: This posture stretches and flexes the spine, with the core connected. Benefits the shoulder, neck, spine and abdominal regain.

1. Stand upright with your feet wide apart and hang arms loosely by the sides of the body.

2. Relax, inhale and take the left arm above the head, with the fingers pointing the sky. Stretch through your fingers, keeping the arm straight.

3. Exhale, and bend to the right, keeping your pelvis in place. Let the head and arm follow the spine.

4. Inhale and float back up to center, keeping your arm extended.

5. Exhale and let your arm flow back down by your side. Slide your shoulder blades, back into neutral, making sure there is no tension in the head, neck and shoulder complex.

6. Repeat the movement to the left with your right hand. Do a total of 5 side bends on each side.

GARDENING WORKOUT

Exercise is a process of continuous movement of the body, after which a person feels fresh and alert because of increase in the blood circulation. Activities like gardening, swimming, sports, jogging, skating, cycling etc are also work-out exercises. You can plan your work-out according to your aptitude and follow it regularly to get best health benefits.

Gardening is a low key activity but one that's been found to improve all-round fitness. It's surprisingly a health punch for women over 50. Gardening appears to help in bone crippling disease osteoporosis. Research shows that only 2 activities such as weight lifting and gardening were important in helping women maintain healthy bone-mass. Gardening's bone boosting benefits are attributed to weight-bearing moves.

Benefits of Gardening: It has been found out, that 30 minutes of moderate gardening each day provides the following health benefits.

1. Lower blood pressure, Lower cholesterol level, help prevent diabetes and also prevent heart disease.

2. Can burn calories, for example a women of 154 lbs can burn upto 331 calories per hour by doing light gardening and yard work.

Research in Horticultural Therapy shows that

1. Putting in a garden, tilling the earth, planting bulbs or seeds, pulling weeds can help reduce stress. We who love gardening are not aware of this major health benefit provided by gardening, we just do it.

   Throughout life I had been doing gardening, it was my pet hobby. But, it is just now that I realized what benefits it gave me. Like any house wife I thought that exercise or going for a walk was just done by those who have time to spare, so I neglected that aspect of my health, but fortunately gardening and household jobs took care of that aspect of my life.

   Gardening kept me active and strong physically and mentally to face the ups and downs of life. Also it kept me slim and trim.

2. **Gardening reduces fat,** it is said to burn as many calories as a 3½ mile brisk walk. It also builds strength, flexibility and agility. Gives relief to pains and stress.

Consider some points before starting gardening:

(i)   Gardening requires bending and for that you should strengthen your hamstrings and your lower back by doing stretching exercises. If you are leading an inactive life, it becomes common to feel achy when you become active again, especially if you're over forty. If, you have not done gardening for a while or have never gardened, practice safe habits.

(ii)   Even while starting gardening, pulling weeds in the garden you pull your back muscles too, or you may feel a twinge in your knee or throbbing in your shoulder i.e. muscles may have stiffness or injury. You can rectify this, the injury is not inevitable and you should not be less active.

(iii)   Stretch your muscles before you start gardening, to prevent stiffness or injury.

(iv)   Wear sunscreen, drink water, to stay hydrated.

(v)   Be careful if you attempt to lift any heavy article.

(vi)   Increase in abdominal pressure can bring on an attack of heartburn, so try to maintain a kneeling position, rather then bending over, while working the earth.

(vii) Wear comfortable loose fitting clothes (no tight belts).

Back is the gardener's weak link, the points below will help to rectify this:

(i)   Avoid carrying heavy loads (weights) as far as possible, especially during gardening.

(ii)   Vary your chores so that you use muscles in different ways and get a full body workout. To prevent fatigue on one side of your body, switch sides when you're weeding or working with a hoe or rake.

(iii)   Don't increase the length and intensity of activity in the same workout. Don't do too much too soon.

(iv)   While gardening, if suddenly, your back starts to ache, stop the activity and rest for the day, but do not stop for long time. Start your active routine again slowly. If, pain continues, take pain killer and start gentle stretching back exercise. Once your back pain is controlled, start your routine in full to make your back muscles strong.

(v)   Avoid bending, unnecessarily do not turn abruptly, so as to protect your joints from overuse. Sit straight.

WALKING FOR WELLNESS

To start off on the right foot observe the following points:

1. Walk straight with your head held high. Keep your whole body relaxed and your hands in a soft fist. Occasionally shake your arms to prevent shoulder tension.

2. Use your arms to increase the cardiovascular benefits of your walk. Bend them at a 90° angle at your elbow then pump your elbows forward and backward, rather than across your body.

3. Hit the ground heel first and roll through, pushing off with your toes.

4. To determine your pace, use the talk test - if you're a beginner make sure you're able to comfortably hold a conversation with a partner. As your fitness increases, take faster steps until it's almost difficult to talk- about a mile in 15 minutes. Walk for 20-30 minutes.

> For older people, who have doubts about their capability to do any exercise, walking is one of the simplest and safest ways to stay in good health. Every other health expert recommends it. 20 minutes walk is considered to build up healthy heart muscles, loads you with aerobic benefits, trims fat, builds better bones, cures aches and pains, and exercises most of the 650 muscles in the body.

5. If you've had trouble sticking to a regular exercise program in the past, try walking once a week with a walking group.   Then supplement the group walk by walking alone or with a partner for the rest of the week.

6. Walking is the perfect time to meditate. Notice how you're breathing rhythmically as your feet are hitting the ground. Repeat phrases like 'I am fit' and 'I am strong' in time with your steps.

NATUROPATHY TREATMENTS

COLD AND HOT THERAPY

The hottest and coldest temperature should be that which you can tolerate on an irritated area. If there is a dull or sharp pain in a localized area, apply ice pack to it in 10 minutes interval, i.e. apply ice on the area for 10 minutes then remove it for at least 10 minutes. Repeat 3-5 times.

Precautions: Icing for more than 12-15 minutes on a specific area will increase the body's natural reaction to increase blood circulation (dilate the blood vessel) in order to protect the tissue from cell damage. The increase flow to the already inflamed area will make it even more inflamed, thus it will counteract by causing more pain.

Cold & Hot Therapy Used for Ailments:

1. *Muscle Stiffness*, use a heating pad or, better yet, take a warm shower.

2. *Injury and Broken Bones:* Ice packs gently laid over fracture or broken bones, will reduce swelling, inflammation and pain. Do this every 20 minutes every 2 hours if the swelling is very much.

3. **A traumatized area** can be treated **with both cold and hot therapy.** Simply, **alternate cold with heat,** for a couple of days if the area is not responding to either alone. This can also be done once the pain of an acute injury has been reduced.

The Reason Behind the Alternative Therapy is: Ice constricts the blood flow while the heat promotes blood flow. When you alternate between two, you will help accelerate the removal of pain producing waste products in the injured region. Always begin and finish with cold application.

The two standard methods of hot and cold are:

1. Five minutes of moderate cold and 5 minutes of moderate hot temperatures.

2. Twenty- thirty seconds of very cold and hot temperature. Do not make the hot temperature over 105°F (40°C).

Warning:

1. Hot or Cold temperature should never be applied to area where there is reduced sensation. This may make you apply hot/cold without realizing the damage being done.

2. It should not be applied to area where there is a chance of infection or malignancy.

3. Cold is not recommended for people with peripheral vascular disease, such as sickle-cell anemia or Raymond's disease. **Naturopathy** relies on the controlled effects of hot and cold water on the body.

Naturopathy - a simple remedy...

1. ***Steam Inhalation:*** This is good **for a bad cold, when the ear block, and sniffing and coughing would persist.** Steam inhalation for 3 minutes followed by a cold compress for a minute, around the temples, forehead, cheek and nose. This procedure is to be done 3 times at one sitting, thrice during the day. You can be sure that it works.

2. ***Hot water tubs*** can massage sore muscles, give relief to joint stiffness, restore flexibility and enhance sleep. Thirty minutes of soaking every day in hot water tub can lower blood sugar levels in type 2 diabetic patients.

3. ***Cold Green Soak:*** **Minor burns formed by exposure to sun or while cooking** can be treated with a cold compress of black or green tea. Soak a dish towel or a face towel in cold tea and dab it on the affected area. The phyto-nutrients will reduce the inflamed blood vessels.

4. ***Hot & Cold Shower Therapy or Hydro-therapy:*** This therapy was based on hot and cold showers, rinses, baths and compresses. The treatment aims to increase blood flow, stimulate the metabolism, tamper pain and boost immunity.
   Water applications benefit not only the blood vessels, but also the nerves as 90% of our autonomic nerve endings are in the skin's surface. Hot water especially has a stimulating effect on the nervous system, relieving stress and insomnia symptoms.

5. ***Salt Water Bath:*** Stir ½ kg of table salt in 100°F bath water, soak your body in it for 20 minutes, then take a cold water shower, rest for 20 minutes. Repeat this bath every 3rd day for 6 weeks to get the best results.

6. ***Cold Therapy for Fever:*** Wrap the calves first with a cool, damp linen and then with a layer of dry linen and then with 2 layers of cotton cloths and 2 layers of wool cloths. The wrap can be repeated every 15 minutes to lower the fever.

   A cold water wet hand towel when placed on the forehead of the patient can also reduce the fever. The wet towel should be changed every time the cool towel becomes warm on the forehead. Continue till the fever comes down, will take approx. 10-15 minutes.

7. ***Soothing Sore Joints:*** Heat can give relief to the stiff joints. Stiffening your joints and limiting your mobility in Osteo-arthritis is due to the break down of cartilage, which is the cushion between the bones, causing the bone to rub against bone. Your body can repair cartilage if it gets what it needs. ***Quick Methods for Relief are — Hot and Cold Mixing:*** Heating and cooling the joints have a numbing affect on the tissue, and it can also speed healing if there's some sort of inflammation.

   Method: Wet a towel with comfortably hot water, place on the joint. After 3 minutes, replace with a cold wet towel for 30 seconds. Repeat 3 times.

8. ***To Soothe Skin by Mineral Rich Water:*** The treatment with mineral-rich spring water will relieve the pain from burns and rashes. It's also used to treat itching and redness after laser skin re-surfacing. The trace minerals in the water work as anti-inflammatory.

THERAPEUTIC MASSAGE

This is the oldest form of healing known to man. Therapeutic massage uses pressure and motion to your muscles and soft tissues to support circulation, relaxation and sore muscle relief.

Massage: Massage and diet can control practically every disease, specifically rheumatic diseases. Massage can be done on any part of the body including the head, with herbal oil.

1. *Self-massage:* Most people who **instinctively rub their neck or shoulders** when their muscles are sore or tense have no idea that they are using this massage technique. Besides alleviating aches and pains, this is an excellent way for those in good health to **use self-massage on a routine basis to prevent disease.**

> **Self-massage** is a proven remedy for fatigue, insomnia, muscle tension, muscle weakness, joint pain, circulatory disorders and skin problems. It may also help heal an injury, such as a sprain, by bringing fresh oxygen to the affected tissues.

For Self Massage: loofah - dried fibrous residue of the cucumber relative Luffa cylindrical, can be used in the bath or shower to improve dead skin and also to improve the blood circulation and drainage of the lymphatic system.

Rubbing: To stimulate circulation and release muscle tension, rub your muscles in circular motions with your hands and fingers. Begin each massage by gently stroking the skin. Then, either using one hand or both hands, start rubbing your muscles. While using both hands, move them together or alternate between them. Work the strokes toward the heart.

I rub my painful, slightly stiff knees very gently for at least 100 circular motions with my palms and fingers, both clockwise and anti-clock wise in the morning. This relaxes the knee muscles which results in removing the stiffness and thus the pain.

Kneading: Using a little warm natural vegetable oil like olive oil or mustard oil, as a lubricant, work on your muscles as if you are kneading the bread dough.

I knead the painful parts of my knees for 10 minutes.

Vibrating: Use rhythmic knocking or lightly patting with your flat hands, to improve blood circulation and relax muscles. Finally, end every massage with gentle strokes, slowly moving outward.

Special masseaurs also give a good body massage. But remember to appoint a trained masseur to do the job. Firm massage strokes warm the skin and assist the penetration of oil, takes at least 10 minutes. The massage can be done well over an hour.

Benefits of Massage

* Helps in healing of illness.

* Soothes pain.

* Removes anxiety.

* Benefits arthritis.

* Relief to hypertension.

* Migraine.

* Chronic fatigue.

* Improves blood circulation.

* Increases stimulation of lymphatic system, particularly lactic acid.

* Helps remove toxins that have built up in the muscles causing the stiffness and pain.

* Lactic acid is also built up after strong exercise, for this the athletes as well as tense office workers need massage.

* Massage helps human bonding, improves self esteem and we recognize the healing touch of the hands.

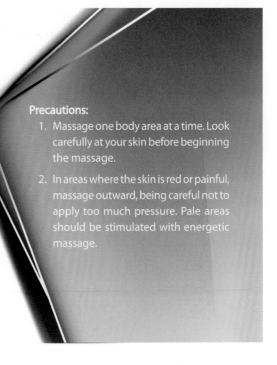

Precautions:
1. Massage one body area at a time. Look carefully at your skin before beginning the massage.
2. In areas where the skin is red or painful, massage outward, being careful not to apply too much pressure. Pale areas should be stimulated with energetic massage.

Massage Therapy Used in Home-remedies: Plant oils such as almond, apricot kernel and wheat germ have vitamins, which can be absorbed by the skin. **Sweet almond oil** contains vitamins F & E which assist nail growth, skin repair and is good for hands. **Apricot kennel oil** contains Vitamin A, which softens hardened skin on the feet. **Wheat germ oil** contains vitamin B. Lotions that contain cooling **peppermint oil** are also good for tired, aching feet.

ESSENTIAL HERBAL OILS

These herbal oils are essential oils that assist in cell regeneration and healing when applied to the skin.

Some of the beneficial effects of massage by using essential oils

(i) **Head and Hair Massage:** When I was ten years old my aunt (my father's sister) was our frequent visitor to our house. She had long, black, shinning hair. I was very fascinated by her hair and asked her how she took care of her hair.

In reply she made me sit in front of her and asked my mother to give her Mustard hair oil. Then she started giving a head massage, she did so well that my head became light, my hair became smooth, silky and soft as if she had combed them with a comb. I follow her massage instructions till this day and the result is that I have soft and more black than grey hair at the age of 76 than most of those in their thirties.

Scalp Massage:

(a) Start your scalp massage at the hair- line at the nape of the head.

(b) Grip scalp firmly with fingertips of both hands and drawing the fingertips together and apart with a slow pinching movement as you push up towards the crown of the head. This brings the circulation to the scalp.

(c) Repeat 2-3 times and then move the fingertips to the hairline above the front hairline and push backwards.

Ayurvedic Oil Massage Treatment for:

1. Cervical spondilitis, Joint pains, gynecological disorders, arthritis, other rheumatic complaints.

2. Mental diseases like hysteria, insanity and hallucination.

3. Physical conditions like Asthma, tuberculosis.

4. Besides the above this can also be effective for polio, paralysis and muscular dystrophy.

5. Migraine, facial paralysis and other nerve disorders are also treated by oil massage.

But this massage treatment is expensive due to the fact that large quantity of medicated oil is required, though no doubt it is an effective age old system.

Benefits: This movement causes actual scalp friction and is excellent for permanent waved heads, falling hair that is inclined to come out easily.

(ii) **Foot Massage with Peppermint Oil Diluted in Vegetable Oil**

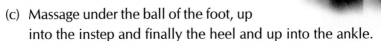

(a) Apply 2-3 drops of oil well and apply the oil to one foot at a time.

(b) Start massaging toes. Pull gently and rotate them one by one then move the foot, the ankle using the hand to massage.

(c) Massage under the ball of the foot, up into the instep and finally the heel and up into the ankle.

(d) End by using both hands over the whole foot from toe to ankle in smooth, continuous strokes. You can feel the blood circulating in the feet, yet the skin feels cooler. Repeat this method of massage with the other foot.

(iii) **Soothing Steam Facial Using Rose Oil**

(a) Wash and clean your face and remove the make up.

(b) Take a sauna facial over a bowl of boiling water for 5 minutes. Cover your head with a towel to keep the steam around your face.

(c) Dry your face and then massage in some almond oil into which 2 drops of rose oil is added.

(d) Using your fingers of both hands, massage outwards from the bridge of the nose, above and under the eyes, outwards across the forehead and cheeks and outwards from the chin along the jaw line.

(e) Finally, massage the neck with downward movements of the palm of the hands towards the shoulders and back.

(iv) **Oil of Peppermint for Tired Face Muscles**

(a) Fill a bowl with boiling water and add 5 drops of peppermint oil.

(b) Cover your head with a towel & bend over the water inhaling the vapors & allowing it to spread over your skin. It will cool tired hot muscles.

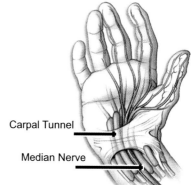

Precautions:

1. Do not use peppermint oil, if you are on homeopathic remedies, as peppermint oil is said to negate them.

2. As these oils are very strong, pregnant women should not use essential oils.

(v) **Massage Therapy for Treating Carpel Tunnel Syndrome**

I had a shooting pain in my right hand, after my first granddaughter, Mehga was born. While playing with her and picking her for long stretches I got this pain. It was so painful that at night if by chance I had to push the comforter a little aside, I could not even bear the weight of the comforter on the wrist and unbearable pain used to shoot up.

Symptoms: This pain in the wrist comes after repetitive lifting and hard work done with the hands. There is tingling & burning sensation and the peripheral nerve compression is the outcome of the repetitive wrist action.

Massage:

(a) Apply a little extra virgin olive oil to the front and back sides of patient's left wrist & hand, with the palm side facing up, begin slowly massaging in a gentle, circular motion with your right thumb and index finger on the flexor tendons and the median nerve located within the carpel tunnel itself.

(b) Turn hand to face the palm down. Grip the patient's hand with your hand index finger while at the same time slightly pushing on the backside of patient's hand with the bent tip of your thumb.

Carpal Tunnel

Median Nerve

(vi) **Massage for Stiff and Aching Joints:** Warm coconut oil or mustard oil mixed with camphor when used for massaging on the stiff and aching joints will give relief.

(vii) **Tired Muscles Massage:** Black Pepper is a warm spicy oil, which is ideal for massage or it may be added to bath water to stimulate the mind and rejuvenate tired muscles.

(viii) **Massage with Herbal Clove Oil for Stiffness of the Neck:** Body ache can be relieved by massaging the body with oil mixed with a pinch of ground clove. This will give relief to even a great pain.

SOME COMMON PROBLEMS

SELF MANAGEMENT AND CARE

DIABETES

Instead of going on a completely sugar-free diet, now beat blood sugar by putting these on your plate...

Apple Peel
Apply peels have sugar reducing powers. They contain quercetin, a flavanoid that has anti-oxidant effects that helps in reducing diabetes. So when snacking on the fruit, remember to eat it whole. Apples come in many varieties. No matter which variety you choose, the benefits are equally high.

Asparagus
Asparagus is an excellent source of glutathione — an antioxidant compound that is known to keep blood sugar stable. The edible parts of the stalk are the shoots that appear underground, so choose those that are tender and green.

Beans
Most members of the legume family contain phytonutrients that are not only good for the heart but will also help you battle diabetes. The best way to take full advantage of these is by consuming dried beans that have been soaked in water for several hours before cooking. Think *rajma*, *chole*, etc.

Oranges
This perky fruit is not just another pretty looker about town. It's packed with phytonutrients that can help you fight diabetes including flavonoids, carotenoids, terpines, pectins and glutathione. It rates low on the Glycemic Index, which means it does not affect blood glucose levels highly, making the orange a good friend to have.

Broccoli

Broccoli is easily available at most speciality food stockists. It is an excellent source of quarcetin which will help you in your war against rising blood sugar. So blanch it for your salad or puree it for the soup.

Carrots

Have you heard of a rabbit with diabetes? It's probably because of all the carrots they munch. Jokes apart, these vegetables are not only good for your eyes, like your mother said, but also full of carotenoids that can help balance your insulin levels.

Nuts

Nuts are power-packed with minerals and healthy fats that protect your heart and balance your blood sugar. Go nuts!

Fish

Another great reason to dump red meat in favour of fish. Not only do the omega-3 fatty acids found in fish help fight depression, they balance your blood sugar levels and protect your heart.

Soyabeans

Also a member of the legume family, the soya bean is a complete source of potein, and also provides phytoestrogens, isoflavones and saponins that can help balance blood sugar.

Tea

Apart from being high on anit-oxidants that act as a cleanser for your system, here's one more reason not to miss out on your daily cup of chai. It has phytonutrients such as catechins and tannins that can help balance your blood sugar.

STRESS

Stress is the main culprit for most of the body ailments. One should know the causes and how to handle them to enjoy a stress free life. Stress could be due to conflicts in life, worries about problems or shortage of time. The body interprets these pressures as a threat to life. Too much stress can cause mental sluggishness and low energy.

These can be reduced by regular exercise and social good relationships. To forget and forgive is the key note to living a healthy and happy life.

Symptoms of Stress

1. Feel irritated and hurried

2. Have trouble in concentration

3. Have a hard time listening to others

4. Now, you don't take much pleasure in things that used to be fun for you

5. You are not able to rest, thoughts keep spinning through your head

Avoiding Stress

1. Take 10 deep breaths and concentrate on relaxing your whole body.

2. Yawning can help you relax by stretching the muscles, increasing the oxygen intake and releasing the tension. Yawn loudly and stretch your arms several times a day.

3. Nuts are a good source of vitamins and minerals that support the central nervous system and cardio-vascular system. These include magnesium and B vitamins. Eat nuts as a snack to combat stress and increase concentration.

4. Relaxation is a great remedy for stress. So people susceptible to stress should make time to doze every day. Lack of sleep leads to exhaustion and decreases your ability to manage stress. Take 6-8 hours complete sleep at night.

5. Massage induces relaxation and emotional well being, strengthening your resistance to disease.

Tips to Cope with Stress

1. There is a link between strong social support network and reduced levels of stress. Maintaining friendships may be effective, particularly for women.

2. Keep busy with the activities you enjoy e.g. reading a book, walking, doing crossword puzzles - these can reduce stress. Any fun activity can lower your blood pressure, and reduce your stress.

3. A good laugh can break the intensity of a situation and give you some much needed perspective. When you laugh your brain releases endorphins that create feelings of joy. A sense of humor is a key facet in creating greater balance in life.

4. A warm bath is relaxing on its own, but the effect is intensified when you add some herbs to the water. Fresh herbs or essential oils can be used.

5. To relieve stress, simply pinch the bridge of your nose briefly with your thumb and the forefinger.

Breathing Exercise for Anxiety

Regular physical activity not only helps improve the way you look, but can reduce levels of anxiety, tension & fatigue – all outward signs of crippling stress.

1. Sit on a chair without armrest, with your feet flat on the floor and thighs parallel to the floor.

2. Hold your back straight. Lay one hand over the other or place palms on your thighs comfortably.

3. Inhale through your nose and breathe deeply without forcing it.

4. Expand your chest fully and raise the shoulders slightly. Breathe in and imagine the air expanding your abdomen and chest in all directions.

5. Then slowly exhale through your nose and make sure that your exhalation took longer time than your inhalation did. Repeat this for at least two minutes. Do it in a comfortable rhythm and do not strain yourself. Stay focused. Breathing deep and full can make the body completely relaxed.

HEART

Exercise is a powerful medicine. Regular physical activity has been shown to reduce risk of heart attack, improve brain functioning, prevents Alzheimer's, stroke & some cancers. Many problems we thought were symptoms of ageing are actually symptoms of disuse.

Changes in the Body After 50's:

1. Upto 50 you get away with not exercising after that, you start paying the price. Unless you do resistance exercise, i.e. strength training, yoga posture, or with weights or elastic bands, you lose six pounds of muscle a decade.

> Heart attacks and most strokes are due to blocked blood flow, usually caused by a clot in an artery. When blood flow to the heart is stopped or reduced, it triggers a heart attack. When the brain is deprived of blood, the result is a stroke.

2. The changes in body composition not only weakens our strength, it also lowers our metabolism and exposes us to greater risk of age related diseases.

3. The loss of muscle and accompanying increase of body mass, puts extra strain on the heart, alters sugar metabolism (increasing the risk for diabetes), and unbalances the healthy lipids in the blood, leading to heart attack and stroke.

Symptoms of a HEART ATTACK

Uncomfortable pressure, squeezing or fullness in the center of your chest that continues for several minutes; pain in one or both arms, back, neck, jaw or stomach; feeling out of breath; breaking out in a cold sweat; nausea; light headedness.

Symptoms of a STROKE

> If any of these symptoms are seen in a person he/she should be rushed to the hospital to take immediate action for control over the illness.

Sudden numbness or weakness in the face, arm or leg-specially on one side of the body; confusion, trouble speaking or understanding; problem in one or both eyes; problem walking or maintaining balance; dizziness or severe headache with no known cause.

ARTHRITIS

If you are going to hurt something, probably it will be your knee. Knee is the site of more debilitating activity - related injuries than any other joint and according to the recent estimates, knee injuries account for more than a quarter of all problems treated by orthopaedic surgeons. For women, the knee joint is even more tenuous - thanks partly to that female figure, making them more prone than men to knee problems.

Osteoarthritis is characterised by degeneration of the articular cartilage and the formation of bony out growth at the edges of the affected joints. There is a common tendency for obese people above 40 to develop arthritis. Every time you move, your knee joint supports your weight, so any extra weight you are carrying equals extra stress. Consider the simple act of climbing stairs, which puts four times the normal amount of stress on your knees. If you are 5 kgs overweight, it's like carrying an extra 20 kgs on your back every time you climb stairs.

Doctor's advice on Knee pain are...

◆ Do not climb up & down the stairs or walk on slopes as it puts much strain on the damage knee joint.

◆ Do not stand on one place for more than 15 minutes and that too, put one foot on the stool when you feel the strain on the knee

◆ Regular exercise can help to reduce joint pain. Try walking or swimming everyday for 10-15 minutes, gradually increasing the amount of time of your exercise.

◆ Try stretching exercises such as yoga for movements and posture.

◆ Wearing shoes that fit well and are designed specifically for the well-cushioned soles reduce stress on weight-bearing joints.

◆ Don't push yourself too hard. Too much exercise—particularly anything that jars the knees, hips or other joints—can lead directly to osteoarthritis. If you experience extra pain, you may be overexerting yourself and should cut back or change to a less physically demanding activity.

The pathological changes in osteoarthritis are difficult to be cured. Analgesics are useful in relieving pain. Rest in bed and reduction of body weight by consuming a well balanced diet is essential.

Your body has the natural ability to heal itself if the proper conditions are established, such as correcting the joint alignment and movement pattern so that you allow the corresponding nerve to function better. Previously doctors, recommended Arthritis patients to refrain from exercise, they thought weight-bearing movements would damage already tender joints. Recently new research shows, **that moderate physical activity can actually be a useful tool for arthritis**. Check your doctor before you start exercise program.

Treat your joint pain and arthritis at home:

Exercise reduces joint pain and stiffness, builds strong muscles around the joints and increases flexibility and endurance. It helps to promote overall health and fitness by giving more energy to the patient. If you are having stiff and painful joints as after a workout, or when sore joints prevent you from workout, a heating electric pad, a hot water bottle, a heating lamp or a capsaicin ointment can help. When your joints become hot, applying some cold pad or a frozen bag of peas-can help reduce swelling by constricting blood vessels. Sleep is also an important factor for good health: Sleep and rest also have radical affect on your arthritis pains.

Yoga Exercise for Arthritis Knee Pain

I tried this and it relieved my pain, due to which I can move up and down the stairs without difficulty within a few days. These are low impact exercises like yoga, swimming and walking which can slow cartilage loss and improve range of motion. You can do this exercise even if you are

Patients should not strain themselves. There will probably be days, when they simply cannot practice at all. So, wait for a day or two until the intensity of the painful period has passed, then begin again. It should be understood that in the cases of exceptional stiffness and arthritis the bad spells are part of the system and that progress is never easy i.e. one takes a few steps forward and one backward.

having pain in your knees, do it slowly and with care. See the difference in a couple of days.

1. Lie on your back. Slowly inhale & exhale through your nose 20 times to relax.

2. Pull your knees towards your chest & place one hand on the back of each thigh.

3. Slowly extent your legs upwards towards the ceiling on an inhalation i.e. breathing in, and then fold them on an exhalation i.e. taking breath out, keeping your hands on the backs of your thighs. At first you will feel pain in doing this exercise, but doing regularly relax the knee joint and your pain will subside.

4. Do this 8 to 10 times. Bring your legs down to rest, straighten your legs, and lay your arms by your sides, palms facing up. Take 20 more breaths to relax.

5. Next raise your arms overhead on an inhalation and slowly bring your arms to the floor behind your head, keeping your arms back on an exhalation. Do this 8 to 10 times. Repeat this sequence twice daily.

Yoga Aerobics in the Shower

The best place to perform your routine yoga aerobics is in the shower. The comfortable temperature (between 83°F-88°F) and buoyancy of warm water is a perfect place **to relieve the pain and stiffness of Arthritis**. If you are doing gentle movements while sitting in a hot tub, keep the water temperature slightly higher. **Water supports joints, encourages free movement and offers resistance, which can help to strengthen muscles.** Heat is recommended for many arthritis sufferers, but not all. So consult your doctor before starting any activity.

Benefits of Shower:

1. In addition to gain flexibility, the warm water helps to increase circulation.

2. The massaging effect of warm water also helps override the muscles protective stretch reflex so that one can get into the stretching or relaxing faster.

3. Shower stretch routine allows you to warm up by washing your body first and it is an effective easy routine which becomes a habit. Thus a daily shower can remind one to stretch every day.

Note:

1. If one thinks bath is slippery you can do stretching exercises somewhere safer, only do it every day regularly.

2. Take time to enjoy the soothing water, when you first step into the hot bath.

3. After exercising, allow some time to relax & stretch your muscles again.

Massaging with Oil keeps Bones and Limbs Healthy

1. Massage maintains muscle tone and releases muscle tension.
2. Oil lubricates the joints and makes them flexible,
3. Massage increases the blood and lymph circulation in the sore muscles and removes toxins like lactic acid and cellular products.

Massage gave relief to my knees. I had difficulty to sit on the ground in any asana, but after doing the stretching and strengthening Exercises, and herbal oil massage, I started sitting for half an hour at a stretch, in Sukhasana.

Knee Pain with Self Healing Technique

My knee pain got flared up when I was showing my 4 years old grand-daughter, how to skip a rope. I took only 3 steps of skipping and my knee gave up. Shooting pain appeared and I could not walk or put my left foot up to climb the stairs, let alone my doing any exercise. Here **Folk-remedy, 'Hot Milk Turmeric recipe'** (see page 28) helped me a lot. I drank this, also took hot water bath, which warmed up my inflamed muscles, and applied Ayurvedic muscular relaxant gel, once at night and then in the morning, and the pain went away soon, leaving me fit to do my regular activities.

Home Remedy for Arthritis

(i)   A diet of only bananas for 3-4 days is advised. You can have 8-9 bananas a day.

(ii) Melt ½ cup of Vaseline in a small steel saucepan over slow heat. Add to it ¼ tsp each of black pepper powder and red chili powder. Stir thoroughly and cool until the mixture congeals. Apply topically to swollen joints, twice daily.

(iii) Make tea from papaya seeds and have 6-7 cups a day for at least 2 weeks.

(iv) Have 1-2 garlic (lasan) cloves or 1 single pod garlic (ek pothi lasan), first thing in the morning.

(v)   Mix 1 tsp of dry amla powder with 2 tsp of jaggery (gur) and have it twice daily for a month.

(vi) Soak 1-2 tsp fenugreek seeds (methi daana) in a cup of curd or water overnight. Have it in the morning on an empty stomach.

(vii) Grind fenugreek seeds (methi daana) to a fine powder. Swallow 1 tsp of it with water in the morning.

(viii) Regularly massage affected joints with neem oil.

Physiotherapist Exercises for the Damaged Knees

Strengthening exercises, proper posture & gentle stretching exercises done for 5 minutes can give relief to the joints and muscular pains, which can also be in the initial stages of arthritis.

(i) Lie straight on your back with arms at the side of the body. Raise your right leg straight, one foot high. Hold for the count of 10. Bring it down. Repeat 10 times.

Lie straight as above and repeat the exercise with the left leg with 10 repetitions.

(ii) Stay in the position as above. Roll a towel or put a small pillow under your right knee. While lying straight try to push the pillow down with your knee, without bending it. Hold for the count of 10. Then release the pressure. Repeat 10 times.

Repeat the above stretch with the left knee with 10 repetitions.

(iii) Sit on the edge of a bed or on a chair with your back straight. Raise your right leg to the level of your bed or chair. Hold for the count of 10. Bring it back to the ground. Repeat 10 times. Now repeat the above movements with your left leg. Initially do these stretches 10 times daily. Gradually you have to increase the number of repetitions and to do them three-four times daily.

Importance Of Diet In Arthritis

We all know that one of the components of some forms of arthritis is inflammation of the joint. It is now believed that various forms of oxidative chemicals, called free radicals, can contribute to joint inflammation. For this particular reason, a great deal of sense is required to make sure that you eat diet rich in fruits and vegetables that contain vitamins, minerals and all other vital nutrients. Since most of the patients are over-weight, a well balanced reducing diet with adequate amounts of vitamins and minerals has been found to be successful in a majority of cases.

- **Vitamin C —** The beneficial results of vitamin C may arise both from vitamin C's antioxidant function and the role it plays in the production of collagen, an important component of cartilage.

- **Vitamin E —** Vitamin E is a very strong antioxidant that appears to protect cellular membranes and cell components from oxidative damage.

- **Vitamin A and D —** Vitamin A and it's precursor, beta-carotene fight the oxidative damage of free radicals and vitamins A and D play a role in the development of strong bones.

- **Omega-3 Fatty Acids —** It has been recently reported that omega-3 fatty acids found in oily fishes like mackerel, tuna, salmon, sardine etc. have an anti-inflammatory effect which can help relieve symptoms of arthritis.

- **Ginger —** Research shows that patients given ginger extract experienced considerably less knee pain while standing & walking.

- **Gelatin —** Gelatin is high in two amino acids proline and glycine, that are critical to building and repairing the cartilage in joints.

- **Celery —** Celery too is an anti-inflammatory agent and source of potassium. Eat raw, three times weekly.

Better Raw or Cooked?

Unlike most other veggies, carrots are more nutritious eaten cooked than eaten raw. Because raw carrots have tough cellular walls, the body is able to convert less than 25 per cent of their beta carotene into vitamin A. Cooking, however, breaks down cell membranes and as long as the cooked carrots are served as part of a meal that provide some fat (vitamin A is a fat soluble vitamin), the body can absorb more than ½ of the carotene.

OLD AGE

It is entirely possible to die healthy and active at an old age only by changing your life-style. Modern research shows that there is no single factor that brings about cellular changes of aging, although a poor diet, environmental factors, and lack of exercise can all have an effect.

Post age 50, everyone experiences reduction in body tissue, particularly muscle mass and bone density and a decrease in the efficiency of the organs.

Research shows that there is a loss of muscle mass accompanied by the aging process: About 7lbs/decade for men and 5lbs/decade for women- cause a slow down in resting metabolism that then causes various health problems. This means a loss of strength in many older adults.

Sleep is a maker of all over well being. Sleeplessness increases hunger and unbalances your metabolism, thus increases the risk of obesity and diabetes. Restless sleep is very common among older people.

A pre-bed time snack of walnuts or milk/yogurt are natural sleep inducers because of the presence of amino acid tryptophan.

Common health problems for those 50 and older include:

(i)   Bone density loss

(ii) Cardio vascular diseases

(iii) Depression

(iv) Weight gain

(v)   Memory loss

(vi) Decrease energy and stamina

(vii) In older men, an aging process is prostrate, where the prostrate becomes enlarged and urination becomes difficult. Other conditions that affect them are

(viii) Type II diabetes

(ix) Osteoporosis

(x)   Arthritis

(xi) certain types of cancer.

In old age you suffer from **backache** when you sit for 2-3 hours or walk for even half a kilometer. This makes your leg muscles pain. As we advance in age we become less flexible and muscles, tendons, bones, joints and ligaments slowly deteriorate.

Once age related health problems develop, if neglected can worsen and make you bed ridden. If you are leading an inactive life, it becomes common to feel achy when you become active again, especially after forty.

Other Old Age Ailments Like Memory Loss and Related Problems can be Remedied by Stimulating Mental Facilities: Exercise helps maintain healthy levels of mood-boosting chemicals in your brain. It is proved that sedentary living can almost be as hazardous to health as smoking.

Exercise for 'Urinary Incontinence': Men lose pelvic muscle tone as they age and can benefit from this exercise. Do this 3 times a day, squeeze the muscle of the pelvic floor as if stopping the flow of urine, hold for 20 seconds then take a break of 10 seconds. Repeat 3 times.

Keeping your mind busy and solving challenging problems like doing puzzles, learning a new language, reading and writing, playing cards, any sort of activity which keeps your mind working.

Points for maintaining healthy pain free body:

(i)   Early to bed and early to rise is the first step towards good health, clear sharp mind and a long life.

(ii)   Eat your food slowly, chew each bit at least 23 times and don't keep the next bit of food in your hand while chewing. Drink water or any liquid sip by sip. Eat on regular timings and always eat less than your appetite i.e. don't over eat but always leave some space in the stomach.

(iii) You should take control of your food choices and get on the road to health and longevity, with a diet and nutrition program. The healthy diet has proteins, fruits, vegetables, cereals and other grains and dairy products.

(iv)   Too much stress is harmful, yet stress is there at least to a degree. Our reaction should be to try to make the stress go away. To some extent your stress can be taken care of by what you eat.

(v) Refrain from smoking and drugs. Do meditation for at least 15 minutes, which will control blood pressure, mental stress, heart diseases, psychological problems and cancer.

(vi) Do warm up exercise, at least for fifteen minutes, like running, brisk walking, gentle yoga exercise like sun salutation (surya namaskaar). This keeps your lungs healthy and normal blood flow in the body. Exercise, helps you not to over eat, talking less, saves your time and money spend on medicinal and consultation. If you are not athletic type, then you try walking instead of exercise. You don't have to exercise every single day. Four times a week is good enough.

For starting exercises or any activity, understand the limitations of your own body and never over do it.

(vii) Daily practice of Yoga asana, in correct sequence eliminates toxic chemicals from the body and thus cures constipation. Exercises such as tai chi, Qui gong, and yoga are thought to ease tension and calm the mind. They strengthen muscles and improve balance, which relieves stress on inflamed joints.

(viii) Pranayama has the capacity of freezing the mind and body from painful and unpleasant feelings and thus the physical pain is reduced.

To Keep Healthy, Follow Some Rules:

1. Do not sleep on your stomach, lie on your left side with knees bent.

2. When in a car place a pillow behind your neck to provide support.

3. Avoid cradling the receiver of the phone between your shoulder and neck.

VITAMIN E — The Fountain of Youth

The most powerful strategy you can employ to get vibrant skin is to pursue optimal health. All the make up you put will never cover up the effects of missing nutrients. Like any other part of the body, your skin requires an abundant supply of nutrients to look and feel at its best. Vitamin E is one of the potent antioxidant nutrient that combats the effect of free radicals and acts like nature's preservatives, slowing or reversing ageing. **Vitamin E** keeps your skin and hair looking **healthy and vibrant**. But this wonder vitamin is also an active agent that helps **slow down the ageing** process and increase your immunity. It helps in the formation of red blood cells and the utilisation of vitamin K. It may reduce the risk of certain cancers, coronary artery disease, may prevent or delay cataracts.

Vitamins E is a fat soluble vitamin and exists mainly in fatty foods so it is impossible to benefit from it's cancer-fighting and immunity boosting protection from food alone. It is best therefore to take in the supplemental form. Unrefined vegetable oils, nuts, seeds, leafy greens, almonds and olives have vitamin E but only enough to help manage their own unstable fatty acids.

How Vitamin E Slows Ageing

Antioxidants like vitamin E, including beta carotene and Vitamin C are some of the most important anti-ageing nutrients. When your body performs normal processes like metabolism and detoxification (breaking down toxic chemicals), your cells give off by products called free radicals. These are highly reactive agents that can cause chemical chain reactions causing death of healthy body cells. While the demise of a few cells won't be lethal to the person who is losing them, damage will accumulate over the years. According to some scientists, it is this accumulation of cell death that may be the cause of many of the degenerative processes that we call ageing.

The Brain and Heart Helper

Vitamin E prevents oxidation of vitamin B complex and vitamin C. It is an active agent in the prevention of brain and artery damage. It also reduces the risk of heart disease and angina, which is a severe pain in the heart muscle that occurs when the heart doesn't receive enough oxygen. According to a new finding, **vitamin E** helps keep blood from clotting too easily, which allows it to flow through narrowed coronary arteries.

Other Benefits of Vitamin E

It cleans the arteries & **thins the blood** thereby lowering your chances of a **heart attack**.

This wonder vitamin also removes excess **calcium** from the hardened arteries and transfers it equally to the **fragile bones**.

Few know that Vit E actually helps blood vessels and works like a **diuretic** therapy and **reduces blood pressure**. You can start with 100 IU a day and slowly increase your intake to 400 IU a day. But be careful, if you take in excess, Vit E will raise your blood pressure. Therefore consult your doctor about the dosage before taking it.

Vitamin E increases **stamina** and endurance by helping muscles and their nerves to function even with less oxygen. It is vital for people living in big cities to take vitamin E, as it protects the body against environmental pollutants in air, water and food.

For **women**, vitamin E is essential as it prevents **menopausal symptoms, pre menstrual pains and even varicose veins**.

Vitamin E Guidelines

Vitamin E supplements are best taken with meals that have some fat in them unless one is taking a "micellized" or water soluble form.

Every one should take vitamin E, especially those who smoke. Optimal intake ranges from 400-800 IU per day.

Vitamin E may cause a slight increase in blood pressure in hypertensives. Those with high B.P. should ideally take it under some medical supervision.

Vitamin E thins the blood, so anyone taking blood thinning medication should take vitamin E under medical consultation.

Those on ultra-low fat diets or with fat absorption problems should use micellized vitamin E.

What Else to do for Checking Free Radicals

Antioxidants like vitamin E can only limit the amount of free radical damage to our cells - they can't stop it completely. They will always deteriorate our bodies to some degree. There is something else that is even more important than getting a lot of vitamin E - preventing the formation of free radicals in the first place.

- ◆ **Exercise:** Cells give off fewer free radicals when the body is regularly exercised as exercise puts more stable oxygen in your tissues. Poorly oxygenated tissues are actually more prone to damage from free radicals than those with healthy amounts of oxygen.

- ◆ **Get Enough Sleep:** Melatonin is a hormone released when you sleep. It is one of the most powerful scavengers of free radicals ever discovered. A sound sleep is so restorative that it not only allows for tissue repair but for free radical damage as well.

- ◆ **Eat yoghurt:** Indulge in sugar free, plain yoghurt on a regular basis with a small amount of fresh fruit added to liven it up. These fermented dairy products contain modified fatty acids which stops the progression of free radicals, the way a brick stops a line of falling dominos.

- ◆ **Eat Enough Protein:** Protein is made up of amino acids from which we make some of our most important amino acids. Glutathione, one of the most powerful free-radical neutralising substance in our body is a combination of three amino acids. It not only scavenges free radicals but also helps eliminate a wide variety of damaging toxins that create them.

- ◆ **Drink Plenty of Water:** When you are gobbling up the healthful foods, don't forget to wash them down with a big glass of water. To maintain a healthy fluid intake, wet your mouth with water whenever possible.

- ◆ **The Forgotten Nutrient:** Laughter helps get rid of allergies and keeps them at bay and also releases a stress relieving hormone. Nothing makes you feel better than a good belly laugh; it adds years to your life, makes those worry lines disappear.

- ◆ **Eating a Lot of :** Fresh fruits, veggies, consuming foods rich in bio-flavonoids, tocopherols, polyphenols and other nutrients should be a universal practice.

CONCLUSION

In conclusion, I would like to share a few of my thoughts with you:

I believe in the Chinese Philosophy of going to the doctor WHEN YOU ARE WELL — so that you can keep on being well, and prevent any potential problem from becoming serious!

With this in mind, we can make a determined effort to follow a healthy lifestyle to keep our bodies in top condition. For this I have given suggestions about diet and exercise.

However, illness will attack us from time to time. If it is a simple problem, the first line of action is to try self healing and home remedies, as I have explained.

On many occasions I have gained a lot of useful and practical knowledge from talking to friends who have the same problem that I may be facing. It is in this spirit, in friendship, that I am sharing my own practical life experiences with you, the Reader.

THE SERENITY PRAYER

God grant me

the Serenity to accept the things I cannot change,

the Courage to change the things I can,

and the Wisdom to know the difference.

Sincerely

Swadesh Kohli

HEALTHY RECIPES
BY
Nita Mehta

India's No.1 Cookbook Author

WALNUT & BROCCOLI SOUP

The very healthy broccoli, rich in calcium and anti-oxidants is combined with the omega 3 rich walnuts. Cinnamon has a soothing effect which relaxes the nerves.

Serves 4

2 tbsp walnuts - chopped
1 small broccoli - break into tiny florets (2 cups florets)
1 cup chopped spinach
1 tsp oil, 1" stick cinnamon
3 cups water
1 cup milk
1 tsp salt and ½ tsp pepper, or to taste
a few drops of lemon juice, optional

1. Heat 1 tsp oil in a deep pan. Add cinnamon. Wait for a few seconds. Add broccoli and spinach. Cook without covering on low heat for 3-4 minutes.

2. Add water and bring to a boil. Simmer on low heat for 5-7 minutes till vegetables turn soft. Remove from fire and let it cool down completely.

3. Grind walnuts with ½ cup milk to a smooth paste in a small grinder. Remove the walnut paste from grinder and add the remaining milk to it. Keep aside.

4. Grind broccoli and spinach along with the water into a smooth puree. Strain puree. Mix walnut paste to broccoli puree. Boil. Simmer for 2 minutes. Add salt and pepper to taste. Remove from fire. Add lemon juice before serving.

SPINACH ORANGE SALAD

A delightful green salad. You can substitute spinach with lettuce too or use a combination of both. Fruit adds texture and taste to the salad.

Serves 4-6

200 gm spinach (choose a firm & fresh bundle with small leaves), 2 firm oranges

DRESSING
1 tbsp olive oil, 1 tbsp vinegar, ½ tsp light soya sauce
½ tsp salt, ½ tsp pepper, ½ tsp sugar free powder

TOPPING
2-3 almonds - cut into thin long pieces

1. Trim the stems of spinach. Soak the spinach leaves for 15 minutes in a bowl of cold water to which ice cubes are added. Remove from water and pat dry on a kitchen towel. Tear into big pieces.

2. Remove the fibrous covering from each segment of orange. Keep aside.

3. Mix all the ingredients of the dressing in a small spice grinder or with a whisk till the dressing turns slightly thick.

4. Toast the almonds in a microwave for 2 minutes or on fire in a pan till fragrant. Cut almonds into slices.

5. At the time of serving, pour the dressing over the spinach, toss to mix well.

6. Lightly mix in the oranges. Remove the salad to a shallow flat bowl, top with toasted almonds. Serve immediately.

ZUCCHINI OAT CRUNCH

All the goodness of oats packed in zucchini pieces.

Makes 8-10

1 (500 gm) thick, big, zucchini

MARINADE

½ tbsp garlic

½ tsp salt

2 tsp vinegar

1 tbsp olive oil

FILLING

1 tbsp olive oil

½ cup oats

4 tbsp finely chopped carrots

2 tbsp finely chopped onions

1 cup milk

½ tsp *garam masala*

¾ tsp salt

½ tsp pepper

2 tbsp fresh coriander chopped

1. Cut zucchini into 1½" thick, pieces, about 8-10 pieces. Scoop out each piece carefully with a melon baller keeping the base intact. Chop the scooped zucchini and keep and aside.
2. Mix all ingredients of the marinade. Brush all the zucchini pieces, inside and outside with the garlic and oil marinade. Keep aside to marinate for 15-20 minutes.
3. Heat 1 tbsp olive oil, add onion and saute till soft. Add oats and saute for 2 minutes till light golden. Add milk and stir till thick. Add the chopped carrots and scooped and chopped zucchini. Add garam masala, salt and pepper. Stir for 1-2 minutes.
4. Fill the marinated zucchini with the filling nicely.
5. Keep the stuffed zucchini on the greased wire rack of the oven and bake in preheated oven at 200°C for 20-25 minutes or till soft.

PANEER CHILLA

Protein rich pancakes.

Makes 10-12

BATTER

1 cup yellow *moong dal*

2 green chillies - chopped very finely

1 tsp cumin seeds (*jeera*)

3-4 flakes garlic - chopped

ADD LATER

1 tsp salt

2 tbsp green coriander - chopped very finely

1 tbsp gram flour (*besan*)

FILLING

150-200 gm paneer - cut into 2½"-3" long fingers

2 tbsp finely chopped coriander leaves

2 tbsp olive oil

½ tsp *garam masala*, ¼-½ tsp salt

½ tsp *degi mirch* or red chilli powder

1. Soak dal for 3-4 hours only, not overnight.
2. Strain. Grind along with green chillies, cumin seeds and 3-4 flakes garlic to a smooth paste. Add salt and coriander. Beat well to make it light, adding about 1 cup water to get a batter of a pouring consistency. Keep aside.
3. Prepare the paneer filling by heating 2 tbsp olive oil in a non-stick pan. Add ¼-½ tsp salt, garam masala and red chilli powder. Remove from heat. Add paneer pieces and coriander. Mix paneer with the olive oil. Return to heat, saute for a few seconds. Keep aside covered.
4. Mix gram flour with the batter and beat well. Add 1-2 tbsp water if the batter appears thick. Check salt.
5. To make the chilla, heat a non stick tawa (griddle), lower the heat, spread 1 tsp olive oil with a brush in the centre. With a small kadchhi put moong dal batter on the tawa. If using a big kadchhi, pour only half kadcchi of batter.
6. Spread the batter into a thin round pancake. Let it cook for 2 minutes on low heat till the edges turn brown.
7. Put some oil on and around the pancake and turn it with the help of a flat spoon. When cooked, turn pancake and place 2 paneer slices to get a long piece. Roll up the pancake with the paneer inside. Serve hot with chutney.

CUCUMBER ROLLS

Light & delicious. Enjoy them any time of the day.

Serves 8-10

1 thick large green cucumber

2 tsp sweet mango chutney, available ready made

3-4 cheese slices

8-10 jalapeno slices

20 sliced black olives

a few tooth picks

MARINADE

1 tbsp extra virgin olive oil

2 pinches of salt and pepper

1. Peel cucumber with a peeler from all 4 sides, leaving the centre seedy part to get 18-20 long strips with a green peel on the edges.
2. Place in a flat dish. Sprinkle all the ingredients of the marinade and mix well. Keep aside for 15 minutes.
3. Place a cucumber peel on a flat surface or a chopping board. Place another peel slightly over laping it lengthwise to get a broader strip.
4. Spread just about 1/8 tsp mango chutney on the slices. (The rolls should not taste sweet).
5. Cut a cheese slice into 3 pieces. Place one piece over the cucumber slices.
6. At the end of the strip, place a big jalapeno slice and top with a sliced black olive.
7. Roll the cucumber strip and secure with a tooth pick with an olive slice inserted in it.
8. Place on a serving platter and loosely cover with a wrap or invert a 2" high dish over it and refrigerate till serving time.

SAUNFIYA BHINDI

The green vegetable cooked with a different flavour.

Serves 4

300 gm lady fingers (*bhindi*)
4 tbsp gram flour (*besan*)
4 tsp cumin powder
2 tsp coriander powder
2 tsp fennel (*saunf*)- crushed to a powder
2 tsp dry mango powder (*amchoor*)
1½ tsp *garam masala*
1½ tsp red chilli powder
1½ tsp turmeric powder
1½ tsp salt, or to taste
4 tbsp olive oil
½ tsp fennel (*saunf*)
1 tsp nigella seeds (*kalaunji*)
1 tsp cumin seeds (*jeera*)
2 green chillies - whole

1. Wash, cut both the ends of lady fingers and slit in between.
2. In a mixing bowl put gram flour, red chilli powder, cumin powder, coriander powder, powdered fennel, dry mango powder, garam masala, turmeric powder, salt to taste and 1 tbsp olive oil and mix well.
3. Stuff this mixture in each lady fingers.
4. Heat 3 tbsp olive oil in a pan or a big kadhai, add fennel, nigella seeds and cumin seeds, when fennel starts to change colour, add lady fingers and whole green chillies. Mix well. Cover with a lid and cook on low heat for about 10 minutes till soft.
5. Uncover and cook lady fingers for about 10 minutes till it turns crisp. Serve hot with roti.

PALAK PARANTHAS FRIED WITH MILK

No oil! Milk is used for frying these healthy paranthas.

Serves 3-4

FOR DOUGH

½ cup whole wheat flour (*atta*)

½ cup oats - grind to a powder

¼ tsp nigella seeds (*kalonji*)

½ cup milk, enough to fry

FOR THE FILLING

250 gms spinach (*palak*) – finely chopped (2 cup)

¼ tsp carom seeds (*ajwain*)

1 tsp ginger, garlic

½ tsp chopped chilli

2 tsp curd (*dahi*)

50 gm paneer - preferably home made & mashed

¼ tsp salt or to taste

1/8 tsp red chilli powder

¼ tsp dried mango powder (*amchoor*)

1. Make dough of powdered oats, whole wheat flour and nigella seeds, using enough water to get a firm, soft dough. Cover and keep aside.
2. Heat a non stick pan. Add ajwain and roast the till light golden. Add ginger, garlic and chopped chilli. Stir and add curd. Sauté for 1-2 minutes. Add chopped spinach and cook till dry on medium flame. Add salt, red chilli powder, amchoor and paneer. Cook for 1-2 minutes till dry. Remove from pan and keep aside to cool.
3. To make the paranthas. Divide the dough into 3-4 balls. Roll out each ball into a small circle, place the filling in the center and collect from all sides to enclose the filling. Press over dry flour and roll into medium sized paranthas
4. Heat a non stick tawa. Cook paranthas on both sides on medium heat till lightly cooked. Spread 1tbsp milk on both sides and cook till crisp and brown patches appear. Serve hot.

GULAB KI KHEER

Fresh and fragrant rose petals add an exotic touch to this low calorie Indian dessert.

Serves 6

1 kg milk, preferably skimmed milk, 4 tbsp tukda basmati rice - wash nicely

4 tbsp sugar, 1½ cups fresh rose petals - wash well

2 tbsp water, 1 tsp rose water or a few drops of rose essence

1. Boil milk with rice in a heavy bottom deep kadhai. Cover and cook on medium heat for about 15 minutes till the rice is cooked. Uncover and cook for 15 minutes till you get the desired consistency. Remove from fire.
2. Boil 4 tbsp sugar with ¼ cup water till you get a thick sugar syrup, for about 5-7 minutes. Remove from fire. Add rose petals. Mix well. After it cools slightly, grind roughly in a mixer.
3. Add rose mix to the kheer and mix well. Add rose water. Serve chilled.

BEST SELLING COOKBOOKS BY

Cookbook for Festivals of India

101 Recipes for Children

Tandoori Cooking in the Microwave & Oven

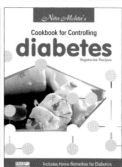

Cookbook for Controlling Diabetes

Step by Step Chocolate Cookbook

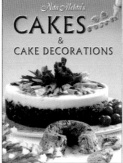

Cakes & Cake Decorations

Zero Oil Cooking

Cooking for Growing Children

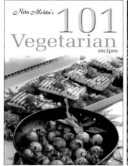

101 Vegetarian Recipes

Indian Favourites

101 International Recipes

101 Microwave Recipes

The Best of Microwave Cooking

Lebanese cooking for the Indian kitchen

101 Diet Recipes

Flavours of Indian Cooking